## Praise for My Millennials

"The author clearly loves her children and has a strong desire to bridge the gap and the many distinguishable differences amongst the generations. I highly recommend *My Millennials* for parents, family members, and anyone in the workforce. This book is impactful and full of insight for the betterment of us all. Anyone who reads this book will gain a better understanding of the life of a millennial."

Wendy Ditta
Best-Selling Author of *The More I Learn, The More I Love*

"In her brilliant and heartwarming debut, Nisreen Khalaf lovingly asks each of us to spend some time behind the lens of the millennial generation and to gain a new and valuable perspective for moving our planet and ourselves forward. Powered by a mother's love and a heartfelt desire to understand and help her own children to thrive in the world, Nisreen has given us a remarkable gift and a beautiful guide for conscious parenting and conscious living. This book will stand up against the sands of time and be counted as a guiding light that leads us all to a place of greater understanding, compassion and empowerment in our relationships with millennials and all human beings."

Michele Marie Neyers, International Bestselling Author of
*3 Lines 30 Days – Unleash Your Inner Poet* (2018)

"*My Millennials* highlights millennial perspectives and the challenges they face as a generation in their academic pursuits, careers, and relationships. Nisreen provides a platform for millennials to share their experiences and world views to help bridge the gap between generations and shed light on how to improve existing systems by considering shared millennial mentalities. Nisreen collects and assesses what makes this generation tick, encouraging understanding and thoughtful coexistence."

Cynthia O'Connor
Program Director in Community Health

"So many millennials are given a bad rap, this great book by Nisreen Khalaf highlights their unique gifts and how they need to be better understood from a mother's perspective"

Linda Staheli
Founding President, Global Co Lab Network

Published by
Hasmark Publishing
www.hasmarkpublishing.com

Permission should be addressed in writing to Nisreen Khalaf at P.O. Box 11772 Burke, VA. 22009

Editors: Sigrid Macdonald
Book Magic, http://bookmagic.biz
Dave Falle
dave@hasmarkservices.com

Cover Design: Anne Karklins
annekarklins@gmail.com

ISBN 13: 978-1-989161-58-6
ISBN 10: 1989161588

Hasmark
PUBLISHING

# My
# MILLENNIALS

*A bridge between two generations*

## Nisreen Khalaf

To my three beautiful millennial children:
Dena, Tarek, and Natalie.
I learned from you more than you could have imagined,
and you heard me more than I could have expected.

# Acknowledgments

So many people played an essential role in my life and inspired me to write this book. I never thought of being a writer, although I wrote in journals to myself often as a way to release stress, anger, or frustration. However, I always had a passion for the young generation, whom I not only raised but also mentored, coached, and befriended throughout my career. I always understood millennials and felt young at heart around them. I commend the millennial generation, and I am very grateful for the things I learned from them. Without this innovative generation, I would not have come out of my box and written this book.

I am thankful for my children, Dena, Tarek, and Natalie, who supported me in writing this book and shared their perspectives openly. It is not easy for a child to be interviewed by his or her mother, but my children wanted me to interview them to help me get the message across.

I have been a student of Bob Proctor for more than a year. I attended a number of his seminars and took a 13-month course with him that taught me how to believe in myself, how to set a goal and go for it with no fear, and how to go after my passion. The material that I studied in that period, and the coaching the Proctor Gallagher Institute provided me, changed my life and my children's. I would not be the person I am today if I had not been introduced to this mastermind person.

I am particularly thankful for Peggy McColl, whom I met at one of the Proctor Gallagher Institute events. The moment I heard her speak, I knew that I wanted to be connected to this talented woman. Peggy guided me and supported me in my writing through a fantastic course she provides online. Peggy is a mother who struggled to be the successful woman she is today. She generously shared her experience on how to be a successful writer with her excellent course, which made me just want to write, when I had almost given up.

A special thank you to every millennial, manager, baby boomer, and parent who allowed me to interview them and were generous enough to share their perspective. I also had the pleasure of interviewing and chatting with organizations working with millennials that opened doors and ideas for me beyond my expectations. Thank you, Linda Staheli and her team from Global Co Lab Network. You are doing fantastic work for millennials, which shows how millennials can be committed to a cause they have a passion for and excel at it.

I hope you enjoy reading my personal experience as a mother of millennials and that you get to see what a phenomenal generation we have today, which will lead us to a better future.

# Contents

# Introduction

*A*s a parent of millennials, I want to start by saying to millennials: I get you. It is difficult to raise children regardless of what generation they come from, but the more the world develops and advances, the more parents have to race to keep up. I do not necessarily enjoy today's social media, but I am curious to know what today's generation is up to and why they are obsessed with it. I also want to be modern and minimize the gap between my children and me as much as possible. The only way I can do that is to be part of their daily technology. Honestly, I met many parents who are more hooked on social media than their children are, especially on Facebook. I also know a few parents who decided to create accounts on different social media platforms to monitor their children. One friend of mine said, "I know where my daughter is and what she is up to through her Facebook. She never shares anything with me when I ask her, so I had to sneak up on her." Of course, her daughter ended up limiting her mother's view of her posts, which made the mom go through other family members' Facebook accounts to check up on her daughter. Unfortunately, millennials do not have much of a private life through social media. They tend to overshare with their postings, which enables the world to know what they are up to and judge them accordingly.

Social media stresses me out, and I find myself bored following people who post too much. I am not referring to millennials only. I am also referring to older generations who became very active on social media. When I first started participating in social media, I enjoyed connecting with old friends whom I hadn't seen for decades. It was nice to see where life had taken them and how their children were doing. Then it became an addiction and an obligation. In my generation, friends often gathered: played, talked, socialized, cooked and did many things together. Today, we hang out through social media, and ironically, if we do meet in person, the older generation appears to criticize social media—even though they are so active on it. I started wondering: if so many people are active on social media, yet they do not like it, why the heck are they on it? Once I noticed how much today's technology was affecting me and taking me away from doing better things with my time, I decided to cut down on its use.

Then my experience with millennials and their use of today's technology started to confuse me. I found myself dumbfounded when my child was in middle school. Her friends would come over and spend their social time chatting together on their phones while sitting next to each other. What happened to playing with Barbie dolls and cars? I struggled to understand and accept this situation, but I also knew it was not under my control. This was a trend that I could either accept, and hope to God that it was only a phase, or work around it without criticizing it. As a parent, the more you criticize, the more your children want to do the forbidden to get back at you. At a certain point, the gap between our generation and our children's makes us the enemy. How can we avoid becoming the enemy and become a friend, without compromising our integrity and beliefs? I don't have a magical answer, but I did a number of experiments until I came up with some tips that might help parents and parents-to-be. I also hope that I can help my children and their generation because they will be in our shoes soon; the gap between them and their children will hit them at one point. Isn't this how it goes: "history repeats itself"?

My intention with this book is to share my outlook on millennials. I do not intend to criticize a generation or a workplace. This is why I do not mention the real names of the people I interviewed or the places where they work. I am interested in the millennial generation, and I believe I can speak about them with a modest understanding. At the same time, I do not plan to mask millennials with perfection. They are not perfect; no generation is.

My relationship with millennials started with my three children: Dena, born in 1988; Tarek in 1989; and Natalie in 1998. Raising my children as a single mother was not an easy job, but a parent's job is never easy. I always say: parenthood does not come with a manual. We have to figure it out as we go. In addition to learning firsthand about millennials from my children and the young colleagues I worked with, I also interviewed about twelve millennials from different age groups for this book. I wanted to hear directly from them and represent their thoughts. To bridge the gap between the two generations, I interviewed parents of millennials.

I am sure my parents found similar difficulties raising my siblings and me, but life during my childhood was different from my children's. We grew up more in the streets than sitting in front of a computer or a TV. We were innovative children creating games out of our imagination, and we would play out with the neighbors' kids all day until our parents called us in because it was getting dark. I give credit to my father, who believed strongly in education and always made sure we were on top of our studying. However, my parents and their generation were more concerned about providing for their family than spending quality time with their children. Mothers, at that time, did not do much outside the house; they were mostly stay-at-home moms. Men were the breadwinners; they needed to have jobs and secure incomes to raise large families at that time.

While growing up and becoming a teenager, I had questions and needs. I didn't have the relationship with my parents to discuss any sensitive issues I was facing, let alone to talk about puberty. Often, I wished I had better parents, and used my imagination to picture the ideal parent I wanted to be. Then, I made a promise that when I grew up and had children, I wanted them to feel that they could talk to me and trust me. True to my word, I established a relationship with my children where they always felt they could discuss any topic with me without hesitation.

My relationship with millennials has continued throughout my professional life. Many of my coworkers, who are considered of the millennial generation, have come to me for professional advice. Despite their lack of experience, they have asked the right questions, which one would expect their managers to have already informed them of. They are basic—yet crucial—matters. For example, millennials have asked me many times how to better manage their time and multi task. Also, they were unsure if they were doing the work properly because their managers were not providing them with positive or negative feedback. Consequently, the millennials had to work under stress, with uncertainty and frustration when their work-related issues could have been easily solved. I tried personally—not as part of my portfolio—to give them feedback and answers to their questions to the best of my ability. I realized that all millennials want, in starting their careers, are mentoring and feedback. Then, they will give their best.

Unfortunately, our organizations and companies are not always that invested in their staff, especially in the younger generations. I do not want to see the young generation burnt out at a job they do not like or where they feel unhappy, as I experienced. If, thirty years ago, I had this awareness, I would have been retired by now. My head convinced me that it was too late to fix what time had damaged for me, but my mind told me that I am not damaged. I just lived life until I figured it out. Now, I can provide a shortcut for those around me who are heading toward a promising future by sharing with them what I have learned.

My children are now adults who have joined the workforce. They have no previous work experience and are relying on the knowledge they gained throughout the fourteen or fifteen years of their education. While they were in high school and college, they didn't realize that they were not taught the skills that they needed for the workforce. Today, my children call me to complain about their work, and the young staff at my job complains to me about similar issues. I came up with the idea of helping the young generation by advising them, "Don't allow life to drag you down until retirement." By this, I mean that millennials need to figure out solutions and better ways to create a future, rather than simply to accept life as it is. "I urge millennials to continue to grow, develop, have adventures, and retire when they want, rather than leaving the workforce at some specific "magical age" embraced by my generation.

The United States Census Bureau states that there were 83.1 million millennials, and there were 75.4 million baby boomers by 2015. That comprises a large section of the American population. Imagine when both generations, hand in hand, build a bridge to the generation coming after: Generation Z, or Boomlets.

Let me share with you this beautiful poem by Will Allen Dromgoole entitled *The Bridge Builder*.

> *An old man going a lone highway,*
> *Came, at the evening cold and gray,*
> *To a chasm vast and deep and wide.*
> *Through which was flowing a sullen tide*
> *The old man crossed in the twilight dim,*
> *The sullen stream had no fear for him;*
> *But he turned when safe on the other side*
> *And built a bridge to span the tide.*
>
> *"Old man," said a fellow pilgrim near,*
> *"You are wasting your strength with building here;*

*Your journey will end with the ending day,*
*You never again will pass this way;*
*You've crossed the chasm, deep and wide,*
*Why build this bridge at evening tide?"*

*The builder lifted his old gray head;*
*"Good friend, in the path I have come," he said,*
*"There followed after me to-day*
*A youth whose feet must pass this way.*
*This chasm that has been as naught to me*
*To that fair-haired youth may a pitfall be;*
*He, too, must cross in the twilight dim;*
*Good friend, I am building this bridge for him!"*

This is my objective for writing this book: I want to build a bridge for the millennials to cross to the other side successfully. I hope that millennials, their parents, and those working with millennials, will learn a great deal from reading this, and find it useful in their relationships and in dealing with social media, applying to colleges, and finding good jobs.

# CHAPTER 1

## Mother of Millennials

*"But behind all your stories is always your mother's story, because hers is where yours begins."*

~ Mitch Albom

Raising my three children as a single mom was a challenging, yet rewarding, experience. There was no Internet to help me Google what to do when my child acted in a peculiar way that I was not able to comprehend. I relied on my instincts and the assistance of others—who often interfered and acted as though they were experts on raising children when they weren't. I made the right decision when I had my first child, Dena, and concluded that I would raise her the way I wished I was raised. Of course, the first child is the guinea pig we experiment on in order to do a better job with the second, if you indeed end up having one. I picked up everything that my firstborn taught me and applied it to my second-born.

The journey of parenthood continuously reminded me of my own childhood, and my relationship with my parents. My parents did their best to take care of and provide for my siblings and me. We lived a good, middle-class life. However, I wished my parents were more approachable so that I could have shared everything I was doing, or planned on doing. I hoped that they would support and guide me. That was just wishful thinking; in those days, many parents were less educated and struggled to make ends meet. Often, children did not have rights. Parents frequently believed in disciplining their children by beating the crap out of them;

I had my share. Our parents looked at children as little people who did not understand, but would when they got older. I understood a lot when I got older, but I was not sure if it was right or wrong. I had to figure out my way through life by trial and error. I was exhausted by the time I became an adult.

I became my children's best friend; they would tell me everything. They would share anything that was on their minds at a given moment, and this made me feel great. I felt I provided them with the warmth I craved. Is it hard to be a mother and a best friend at the same time? No. I was still the adult who provided guidance and set down house rules to build character. What being my children's best friend meant to me was offering them a safe space so that they felt that they could always approach me with anything. We would have a truly open form of communication. They would never fear me as some inaccessible authority figure. I achieved that, thankfully.

That being said, I was not a perfect mom. I was a good mom; I did not have a happy marriage, and I was stressed throughout the twenty years of my marriage because of the effort I put in to make it work. Or, at least, that was the excuse I told myself then. Looking back, I understand that fear of change kept me where I was. The proof of that is that I survived the divorce, and it does not feel as though I was ever married.

I tended to my three children on my own because my husband assumed that his business was more important than my nonprofit work. He repeatedly told me that I could be a stay-at-home mom and that he would care for his family. That would have been the easy option for me, but I am glad I kept working and growing to become the independent woman I am today. Of course, I do not encourage divorce, and a single mother's job is exponentially more challenging than that of a married mother. I would have preferred my children to grow up in a family, with both parents, financial stability, and emotional support. But in my situation, I was spending more time dealing with marriage issues than focusing on my children's wellbeing.

My ex-husband lived in a different country following our divorce. Consequently, he was not involved with raising the children during their critical years, when they should not have had to worry about anything— particularly their education.

It took me several long years to realize that I had two full-time jobs: first, my professional job, and second, my job as a mother. I slept very little for many years in order to manage all my responsibilities, and not fail one or the other. I had my temper and moods. Sometimes, I directed them toward my children. But I did learn along the way, and I grew with my children. I also learned how to treat them based on their feedback.

One day, my son Tarek—who was five years old at the time—responded angrily when I asked him a question. I got upset and told him he needed to watch his manners. He replied, "*So should you!*"

I did not know what to say. He was right. I was teaching him how to talk to me and others, without realizing that I was not setting a good example. I used to lose my temper with my children because I was afraid to direct it at the source of my frustration: my husband. I woke up from my trance when it hit me that I was like a bully who gets bullied and takes it out on others. One day I realized that my problem was with my marriage, not my children. They had no choice coming into this world, and they did not choose me as a mother to treat them badly. Today, I see that my bad marriage was solely my decision, my choice, and my fault. I should have looked for a way out sooner and spared my husband, my children, and myself the pain. But I did not. Instead, I kept making excuses to continue being in a relationship that was making my whole family and me miserable.

I wish with all my heart that technology was more advanced during the late 1980s and early 1990s when my two oldest children were growing up. That way, I could have cracked the problems I was struggling with.

One simple example: Tarek used to have problems concentrating and performing well in academics. He always seemed disinterested in studying, which often frustrated me. Sometimes, I would treat him with sympathy. Other times, I would lose my patience and lash out at him. However, when I would put him to sleep, I would see the face of the sweetest boy on the planet and feel terribly guilty. Our frustrating study sessions became a vicious cycle that repeated itself over and over again until I had had enough. I started discussing my difficulties with other parents around me, but no one was going through similar problems. My child was dealing with concentration issues, reading backward, and writing opposite letters or numbers while simultaneously reading them correctly. This mystery remained unsolved, leading to years of frustration and causing my son to think that he lacked the necessary abilities to excel.

In 1994, I started working as an English teacher at a private school. One day, a mother told me that her daughter had severe dyslexia and needed specialized treatment. She explained that I should not review the child's writing, but ask her to read it for me instead, as I would not be able to understand a single word she had written. I looked at the mother with a blank expression, because what she said was frightening. My mind did not seem to comprehend dyslexia. She could probably see the confusion on my face, so she elaborated on the disorder for me. The symptoms she mentioned included reading backward and writing jumbled math numbers—but speaking them accurately. I jumped off my chair when I realized that some of the symptoms were similar to Tarek's. I asked myself, "Is this what Tarek has?"

It sounded scary, and the student's writing looked foreign to me. It was as if the symbols were not of the English alphabet. However, my son did not have that problem—or at least, it was not as severe.

After work, I went to the library to borrow a few books on dyslexia. I started making some sense out of the information and understood that if my son really did have dyslexia, his condition was minor. I could help him on my own. That was a relief to me. The first step I took was to visit his school and talk to his teachers, just the way the mother of my student had. I was not expecting much from the teachers, but I at least wanted them to know my theory, so they could help Tarek to the best of their abilities.

At home, I would invest hours daily tutoring Tarek to help him memorize. We would play games to help him improve his concentration. I would even provide him with incentives for sitting and studying until his work improved . At that point, I had not told other people, or the rest of our family, about the difficulties we were going through, because I was embarrassed and did not want them to think any less of Tarek, or to view him differently.

I kept it to myself for all those years, until one day, when Tarek was twenty-one, we went camping. While sitting around the fire camp, chatting, our discussion turned to his childhood, and I told him about his dyslexia. His reaction was funny: he said to me, "I always wondered why the damn alarm kept going off, and you would tell me I could take a break. But I never understood why you were doing it." I explained to Tarek that the alarm was the break from studying for him and told him he looked forward to the sound of it.

Taking care of my children as a single mother was manageable. But although I received some child support monthly, I struggled financially. My daughter Dena was eighteen at the time of my divorce. The very first thing she did after enrolling herself in community college was to find a job. She supported herself by working as a hostess at a restaurant in Burlingame, near San Francisco. Tarek was sixteen and worked after school at Lucky— a supermarket—as a bagger. It would break my heart to see them working, when they should have been enjoying their teenage lives, but I was proud that work was their idea, and that they felt a sense of responsibility. This made them appreciative of the money they were earning and also made them understand the importance of attaining a college degree to have a better future. I derived tremendous pride from the fact that my children were growing up to be such responsible adults.

My baby girl, Natalie, was no different. She was only six years old, but relatively independent and mature for her age. It made my struggle as a single mom easier. She would watch the Disney channel and be aware of every toy, but would not ask for them until her birthday or Christmas. At that time, I realized that perhaps I was a lucky mother, because Natalie was certainly more mature than I was at her age. I wondered if this applied to her whole generation.

I never imagined that Tarek would become an engineer one day, especially with his dyslexia. I believe that many of our sessions helped him to improve his work. I would often focus on his concentration in our exercises, along with his short memory. We worked on repetition and memorization. He attended Virginia Tech in Blacksburg, Virginia: one of the best universities in the area for engineering. Tarek chose to study Industrial Engineering with the hope that he would get a good job and start earning a good salary. He graduated in 2014 and started applying for jobs, as any new graduate does.

Of course, the process had begun before he graduated, but he started applying intensively after graduation. After three months passed and there was no sign of a job, he started working as a waiter. He worked long shifts to earn a decent income so he could take care of himself until he got a better paid and more stimulating job. He never imagined that it would take so much time. The application process was long, depressing, and strenuous. He reached a point at which he started wondering whether going to college had been a smart choice. At the same time, he was frustrated working in a restaurant instead of working in engineering.

We did lots of online research to see if there was something wrong with what he was doing, or if there was an obstacle standing in his way. Finally, a company contacted Tarek. He did not even recall applying to this firm. After applying for hundreds of jobs, it was easy to lose track. He got the offer and accepted it with no hesitation. He did not stop to think for a minute if this was his dream job, or if he would be all right living in a remote area, where there was no social life for a young man. He just wanted a job to feel good about himself; to know that he had not attained his degree in vain. As his mother, I was thrilled by this opportunity, but at the same time, I was sad. I knew in my heart that he was smart and would do a great job, yet I also knew that he deserved better. He made the best of his opportunity and went away to live alone, with no friends or social life, for more than three years.

Was he happy? Not at all. He did not like the fact that the company primarily employed locals who had been working there for many years. A few of the employees had held the same position for more than twenty years. In addition, they lacked ambition and preferred to live within their comfort zones. Most of the employees were baby boomers, and very few were millennials. Being a new graduate, with ambitions to learn and grow, Tarek didn't feel this was the right place to take him to the next level. After two years of giving it his best, he started applying for other jobs. He thought that since he now had experience, his job opportunities would be better than they were when he graduated. He applied for jobs for an entire year but did not get any offers. Although he had gained experience and had been promoted—a sign of excellent performance—he could not determine why the right opportunity was not forthcoming.

At the age of twenty-seven, my son came to me and said, "I want to quit my job. I'm very unhappy with a 9-5 job, and I cannot see where it will take me. I want to take time off to figure out what I truly want to do and do it." That was not easy for me to hear as his mother. But when he explained to me what was frustrating him at work, I could connect the dots. Although the job was perfect in many respects—a Fortune 500 company, with a good reputation—it was a five-hour drive from Washington, D.C. Many other young people felt the same way as my son in that they disliked the remote location. Tarek wanted to learn and to grow, but he did not feel that the other employees shared his ambitions. I went through the same phase in my professional life, although I concluded that if I quit my job, it would be a sign of weakness and failure. I admired his courage to take such a bold step, and I knew that I was the one who taught him how to make such decisions.

After Tarek quit his job, he would wake up early in the morning, shower, and dress up, as if he were going to work. Then he would begin his day educating himself through books, online courses, and audios on self-development. At the same time, he started working with Dena to launch an online business store. He worked long hours developing the website by watching videos, listening to recordings, and educating himself on how to establish it. The online store launched and has been successful.

Meanwhile, Tarek invested time in understanding what his passions were. He eventually figured out that his interests lay in furniture and home decor. Interestingly, my ex-husband, Wasef, had been in the furniture business for forty years. My son decided to offer his father an exchange: he would help his father restructure his company, and his father would teach him the furniture business. This is where my son is now: learning the industry he loves, while strengthening his relationship with his father—and helping develop his father's business to go global.

# CHAPTER 2
## The Six Living Generations

*"You are the product of other people's habitual way of thinking."*

~ Bob Proctor

*E*ach generation lives according to the circumstances and values of its time, doing what they perceive to be right. There is no "best" or "worst" generation. Every generation comprises a group of people born around the same time, who have been raised around the same places, exhibit similar characteristics, preferences, and values, and have shared experiences of certain events. Generations are different from each other based on various factors, and it is essential to know which generations belong to which eras.

Regardless of which generation people belong to, they can be happy, or they can be miserable, based on the life they choose to live—not the generation from which they come. Each generation experiences certain trends and has its own characteristics.

### The Six Living Generations in America

There are currently six living generations in America. Four of these generations—in some cases, five generations—are working side by side in the workplace. Visualize a household with people from six different generations gathered for a Christmas dinner. I would love to be invited to one of those gatherings to observe the interactions and bonds between family members. Imagine the gap between the lifestyles of the oldest and the youngest generations. The oldest witnessed the development of the generations preceding them, whereas the youngest generation thinks this is what life has always been like.

Each generation has a different life based on exposure to different technologies and circumstances. For the youngest generation, it is difficult to imagine that there ever existed a time when people survived without the use of smart gadgets. On the other hand, the oldest generation finds it difficult to comprehend that there exists a period where people rely on gadgets alone to make their lives exciting and colorful. The oldest generation has seen the transition, and is often amused by the strides in technological innovation that have significantly affected our lives.

*"Every generation inherits a world it never made; and,
as it does so, it automatically becomes the trustee of that world for
those who come after. In due course, each generation
makes its own accounting to its children."*

~ Robert Kennedy.

Here is a glimpse of the six generations:

## GI Generation (The Greatest Generation)

Any person born between 1901-1926 is considered a part of the GI Generation. Some of the children of this generation were born during World War I, which took place from 1914-1918. This generation grew up during the Great Depression and World War II. The GI Generation lasted twenty-six years, the longest of any generation born in the 20th Century.

*The Greatest Generation*, a book by journalist Tom Brokaw, argues that the World War II generation's perseverance through difficult times is a testament to their extraordinary character. Born and raised in a tumultuous era marked by war and economic depression, Brokaw asserts, these men and women developed values of "personal responsibility, duty, honor, and faith." These characteristics helped them defeat Hitler, build the American economy, make advances in science, and implement visionary programs such as Medicare. They are the people who built the nations of the world into economic powerhouses.

All these features of this generation, combined with the circumstances that they had to go through, made the United States a better place to live. This is why this group will always be remembered as the Greatest Generation.

## Mature/Silents

Any person born between 1927-1945 relates to the Mature/Silents Generation. This generation not only grew up during World War II, but they felt the impact of it. Rising civil rights leaders, such as Martin Luther King, Jr., were from this generation. However, the "Silents" are called as such "because many focused on their careers rather than on activism. People were afraid to express their opinions or to speak out. The people of this generation are known as the children of the Korean and Vietnam War. The majority of women stayed home to raise children or to help out in the house. If women did work at that time, they had limited vocational opportunities and mainly worked in occupations such as teaching, nursing, or secretarial work. Men, on the other hand, worked in corporations, often keeping the same job for life.

The job was just a job for many workers in the Silent Generation. They were not likely to take off to India for six weeks to go to an ashram to "find themselves." Often, people born during this period did not expect to love their jobs. They saw a job as a means to an end: a way to support their family and put a roof over their head, not necessarily a path to self-fulfillment. Many had a great sense of civic duty or obligation to stand by their employer, their government, or their family.

This generation grew up in conditions that were complicated by war and economic downturn. From the period of 1929 to 1939, America suffered during the world financial crisis known as the Great Depression. This affected all social classes. Although farmers, business people, and the lower to middle class were hardest hit, even the very wealthy were forced to curb their extravagant lifestyles. This period caused many American citizens to lose their homes and possessions, leaving them starving on the streets.

## Baby Boomers

Any person born between 1946-1964 is generally termed a "baby boomer." The number of babies born after World War II drastically increased, which is where the name term came from. Around 76.4 million babies in the US were deemed to be boomers. In the '70s and '80s, the rock and roll hippies flourished. Women of this generation started working outside the home and generating two-income households. During this generation, black-and-white TV was spreading inside homes and the word "retirement" was first used.

Their increased birth rates make baby boomers a large portion of today's population, and they have enjoyed a period of increasing affluence and a higher level of income than the prior generation. They have seen a surge in consumerism, which has allowed them to spend more money on food, clothes, and holidays. This generation began to fight for social, economic, and political justice. They fought for many disadvantaged groups, which included African-Americans, young people, women, gays, lesbians, American Indians, and Hispanics. During this period, student activists took over college campuses and organized massive demonstrations against the war in Vietnam. Young people also participated in the wave of uprisings that shook American cities from Newark to Los Angeles in the 1960s.

## Generation X

Any person born between 1966-1976 belongs to Generation X, sometimes referred to as the "lost generation." Many of these children grew up in the streets and held the key to their homes (latchkey kids) because their parents were career-driven or divorced. It was the entrepreneurial era. Computers were introduced in middle and high school. It was not usual to work for a company for life, and people changed careers on average seven times. AIDS started spreading, and drugs became a school problem.

Gen X is usually regarded as America's neglected 'middle child.' We don't hear much about this particular group because all eyes are on the slowly retiring baby boomers, as well as the ascending millennials. A recent study has revealed that Gen X is quickly occupying the majority of critical business leadership roles, although they are sometimes unappreciated. They are a generation that has grown up playing video games, spends most of their time shopping online, and uses social media habitually more than any other generation.

## Generation Y/Millennium

Any person born between 1981 and 2000 is a millennial, also known as "The 9/11 Generation." This generation was raised by parents who were mostly present for them and overprotective. They grew up to respect authority. Education mattered to millennials, and the number of educated millennials with master's degrees increased compared to previous generations. However, unlike previous generations, millennials prefer digital literacy, as they grew up in a digital environment. They collect their information and knowledge through social media and the Internet, which makes them desire fast and immediate answers.

Many millennials take a more liberal approach to economics and politics compared to previous generations. This generation has suffered adversely due to the economic and social damage caused by the Great Recession. Millennials are often cited as being more self-assured than past generations; in fact, there was such an emphasis on improving self-esteem for millennials that some of them have grown up with high self-confidence that doesn't necessarily match their actual performance.

Generally speaking, they also have a strong sense of civic responsibility, a healthy work-life balance, and socially liberal views.

The particular term 'millennials' was coined by an editorial in the magazine *Advertising Age* in 1993 for kids aged eleven and younger.

## Generation Z/ Boomlets

Any person born after 2001 is considered part of Generation Z or the Boomlets. They have never known a world without computers and cell phones. This generation is not interested in toys, which is why a number of companies manufacturing toys have suffered, such as Mattel, the manufacturer of Barbie dolls. The parents of Generation Z invest in their children and spend billions of dollars on them, mostly to keep up with the new electronic devices coming out frequently.

This generation is the first genuinely mobile generation. They place a big emphasis on personalization and relevance. In addition to this, Generation Zs are referred to as entrepreneurial and resourceful. Hence, marketers will need to take all of this into account when shaping strategies for this group.

For this book, I will be focusing mostly on millennials and baby boomers. This will further help to bridge the gap between the two generations so that the generations can communicate with each other.

# CHAPTER 3

## *Let's Meet the Millennials*

*"Young people need to be asked what matters, not be told what matters."*

~ Jeff Martin

The habits of each generation evolve with the conditions and circumstances of that generation. This generation is no exception. They just have a new outlook on life and how to deal with things that life throws its way. Millennials are flexible to sustain the daily pressures of modern life.

This is a general perception of the millennials. In this chapter, I will make an effort to explore millennials from every perspective to avoid the stereotypes that are associated with them.

To begin with, let us ask ourselves a question: who are the millennials? Before I start describing who they are, let me tell you who they are not. I have come across a lot of content on social media and other online platforms, which portrays the millennials as selfish, lazy, and addicted to social media and cell phones. Although this is not true in its entirety, some millennials may come across that way—yet, I have seen non-millennials behaving similarly too. Hence, it is not justified to stereotype an entire generation in a negative manner. Did we forget what the '70s and '80s were like? Our parents were devastated when the hippie movement and rock and roll started. People started dressing differently and coloring their hair purple and green. I lived in that era, and I did not act outside the cultural norms. Neither did most of my friends. This simply means that trends pop up in each generation which identify their time.

# Myths and Stereotypes

I would like to mention a video that I came across on the Internet that appalled me. The video, which is titled "Millennials in the Workplace Training Video," portrays a stereotyped mentality that is associated with this generation. The video highlights the pre-assumed negative factors as if they are necessarily true. One of the videos that went viral shows a millennial in the workforce in a meeting with their managers, discussing an important marketing strategy. In the video, the managers are baby boomers, and the young staff member is, of course, a millennial. When the managers ask the millennial employee about his thoughts on a point discussed at that meeting, the millennial answers, "*Um, what? I didn't get your question.*" The millennial is presented as a very stupid person, his hair standing up like an antennae and his clothes too casual for such a formal meeting.

The video goes on to show another millennial sitting in her cubicle. Her boss comes to ask her a question. Seeing that she is filing her nails, her boss says to her, "*Sorry to disturb you. I will come back another time when you are not busy.*" The millennial oozes confidence and flashes a smile before she responds, "*Thank you for understanding.*" Later, that same girl walks into her manager's office requesting a mental health sick leave.

Even though this video was meant to be funny, it presents an unfair description of a generation. This attempts to show that this generation is extremely careless when it comes to working in a professional environment. Millennials are often presented as people who neither work hard nor aim high. This is an extremely biased approach to describing any generation, which is devoid of facts and figures to back it up.

# The Effects of Technology

Millennial's relationship with social media has been stronger than that of any other generation except for Generation Z, and their technical knowledge gives them a head start in their career, rather than causing a setback. Millennials utilize these resources to connect to the world and are more enlightened about their circumstances than other generations. Most millennials have information about what is going around them. This gives them an opportunity to be more perceptive about every change that takes place in the world. They believe in causes and are passionate about social justice.

*"Millennials expect to create a better future,*
*using the collaborative power of digital technology."*

~ Mal Fletcher

The common perception is that millennials are slack in their work due to their extended usage of gadgets, but in reality, technology provides them with a chance to finish their jobs more efficiently and to be more perceptive to the happenings around them.

*"Social media keeps growing, and people chase the*
*latest and greatest. That is the game of it in the world we live in.*
*I don't think you can go backward."*

~ Mark Frydenberg, senior lecturer of
Computer Information Systems at Bentley University

Millennials easily adjust to new devices and operating systems. They are comfortable with the idea of a public Internet life, which means that they are good at self-promotion and at fostering connections through online media.

Also, many millennials have expensive tastes, even though they might not be able to afford the things they so cherish. This may be an exaggeration, but there is some truth to this argument. Also, this generation tends to stay healthier than previous generations. On the flip side, often millennials are impatient and want things to happen instantaneously. They desire more than they can afford. They ultimately desire whatever social media brings to them. Following these trends causes economic stress for millennials, who live the dilemma of wanting everything that social media promotes when they cannot afford it.

One important characteristic of millennials that their parents feel strongly about is that they think skeptically about authority. This is ironic because they are not particularly rebellious, and they do not want to appear aggressive, or willing to defy traditional ways. They want to experiment with new things, rather than following the same rigid path as set by their elders. This approach often manifests as a rebellious approach, but in reality, the underlying intention is that they have certain ways that are different from other generations.

## How Millennials View Work

Millennials are different from any other generation in their understanding of working for a living. They see their work as a calling instead of a job. This conflicts with the attitude of baby boomers, who had a very rigid approach to a 9-to-5 job. Millennials, on the other hand, may quit a job if it fails to fulfill their soul. They feel that a job is not just meant to keep one busy, pay the bills, and keep the ball rolling. They expect their job to give real meaning to their lives. This is a striking feature of this generation that awards them the privilege of being more passionate and having an attitude that involves changing the world. Millennials show up looking to make an impact, be a part of a team, and do meaningful work that will make a difference in the world. They drive companies to challenge the status quo of how the workplace operates. Due to this approach, managers tend to come up with different sets of strategies to retain millennial employees and keep them motivated.

An organization that houses most of the millennial employees will always be on the lookout for new avenues rather than practicing the same old traditional ways that would make an organization run on stagnant strategies. Millennials are flexible employees and can sustain the daily pressures that the modern corporate world has to offer. Although there are many negative myths surrounding millennials, they are known to be the most adaptable and ambitious generation. According to a UK blog article entitled "The Work Habits of Millennials," 35 percent of millennials across the globe have started their own business besides their primary employment to earn additional income.

Also, *Forbes* magazine states that millennials seek a better work-life balance than their parents. They do not prefer working in rigid working conditions like machines, but they are somewhat task-oriented and focused on finishing the task at hand with perfection. They are attracted to flexible working conditions that give them a chance to improve their skills while spending quality time with their families.

Millennials type with their two thumbs faster than I type on a computer. They can access every Google search and app from their tiny cell phones and prefer that to a laptop, or even a tablet. They are the generation of innovation. Most social media, including Facebook, SnapChat, Instagram, and others, were invented and created by millennials (Twitter is an exception to this rule in that the founder, Jack Dorsey, was born in 1976). Although they have more information accessible to them than the previous generations, they see themselves as the lost generation. Sometimes, this generation is lost figuring out how to utilize all the knowledge around them.

Everything happens so fast for this generation that it can cause stress and confusion. I find a new app or device every few months. I learn from my children of the new apps that are trending, and if I see them as useful, I download them too. However, I cannot figure out on my own how to look for new apps as quickly as they do. I see millennials as a generation that is racing endlessly. Every time the race is over, a new one starts, and they have to start the race over again. Millennials are the generation racing through the present moment so that they can rest in some nebulous future. Everything that happens around them, including the technological advancement of their time, has increased the pace of their lives.

I think it is essential to see the significant accomplishments of millennials and what more they can do. I commend them for their creativity and innovative ideas. The way they have used their brains to frame new ideas in practical ways, while creating new avenues for the world to think, is phenomenal. Previous generations have also learned from them. Many millennials look for what people are good at, not what people are weak at. Generally speaking, they do not idolize anyone or want to be like them. I like their way of thinking. I believe that we are unique individuals, and I know each one of us, as humans, is good at something (or many things). This is what we should focus on: to go after our passions and excel.

I mentioned the story of my son with dyslexia. It never stopped him from being the smart man and successful engineer he is today. I derive immense pride from the fact that he became his own inspiration, and nothing stopped him from achieving what he wanted to. Millennials are more inclined to being their own motivation, which constitutes a significant part of their approach to dealing with the problems in their lives.

Dena, my daughter, did not allow grief to stand in the way of her journey to follow her passion for art. In 2016, Dena lost her childhood sweetheart and husband to a tragic accident. Waseem was only twenty-nine years old when he passed away suddenly. They were young, with hopes and dreams for the future. I wasn't sure how she would recover from her grief or what she could be capable of. Although Dena had artistic skills, she never thought painting and drawing would get her far. She approached art as a means of healing her pain. Once she utilized her talent by designing her own products, she became confident and fell in love with what she is doing today. Her work stopped being just a hobby to her and turned into a career. All it took was confidence and passion. These children used their love by turning it into a successful career. People do not need to restrict their passion to their hobbies. They can choose jobs they enjoy and still have a flourishing career.

# Relationships

Another critical trait that this generation exhibits is the prevalence of relationship problems. During the millennial era, finding a compatible partner and the stable relationship that everyone craves can be a tedious struggle. While they juggle to keep a balance between their work and social life, millennials sometimes have difficulty finding the right partner. They sometimes dwell on their professional lives, which makes it more difficult to meet people in real life.

I have difficulty understanding why this younger generation is incapable of finding love easily. Why do they need online apps to find a partner when they should be able to find the right person in their surroundings? I have realized that the online social life of millennials isolates them from physically being around people, so now they get more satisfaction from socializing on social media than in person. In addition to the student loans they owe and the expensive lives they lead, they need to cut down on going out as often and work multiple jobs to earn extra income.

Interestingly, I have met many people who found the right match on a dating website and are happily married. Shena struggled to find the right guy. She dated a few times, but realized that they were not the right match for her, intellectually or maturity-wise. She started feeling insecure about herself and concerned that she would grow old without ever getting married and having a family. She gained weight, went through a depression, and started feeling resentful toward anyone in a relationship. One day, she came to visit and opened up about her feelings. I was impressed by her honesty in admitting her resentment toward happy couples. I asked her lots of questions to understand what made her believe that she had no chance of finding love. (Keep in mind, she is beautiful, highly educated, and very successful in her career.)

When she started talking, I realized she was comparing herself to her friends who were in relationships, and she was thinking they were either luckier than she was or better looking. A few years later, Shena decided to give online dating a try. She said, "You flip a few frogs before you find your prince." She found her prince, and today they are happily married. I guess I can see how these dating sites can solve problems for those who are unable to find the time to socialize and meet a partner. However, I preferred the past, before social media, when people socialized more in person and had a better chance of finding the right match.

According to the documentary "Swiped: Hooking up in the Digital Age," there appears to be a gender difference in online dating preferences. Quite a few men, particularly younger men, are merely looking for hookups, whereas many young women are looking for stable relationships. The great variety of partners online makes it difficult for millennials to choose just one person and stay with them because of the feeling that the grass is always greener on the other side, i.e., that they are missing out on the next best person. Millennials may experiment with relationships more than their parents did. In the long run, as they get older, I hope that many will settle down in satisfying relationships.

*"Unlike previous generations, millennials have grown up in a world full of dating apps. Gone is the day of simply meeting and marrying the boy or girl next door. The sheer amount of choice present in today's dating scene can make commitment even harder for a generation who has been conditioned to have it all."*

~ Tara Griffith, therapist

Millennials derive satisfaction by mingling on social media, but they do not want to go out together to socialize. This creates a gap between the partners; therefore, they may have a hard time keeping up with their relationships. It also makes cheating easier because there is such a vast number of partners to choose from, and a fling is just one click away. In an era where millennials have to keep up with the fast-growing trends of the corporate world and learn new skills to cope with changing dynamics all around them, they have a lot to deal with. This generation likes to challenge everything that society places in their way. Moreover, they want to mold every obstacle in such a way that it becomes a catalyst to take them closer to their goal.

# Millennials Influencing Each Other

*"No one is useless in this world who lightens the burdens of another."*

~ Charles Dickens

Like any other generation, millennials' peers have a strong influence on each other, as well as on other groups around them. Millennials influence one another through social media. Millennials tend to follow the lifestyles of their peers—especially in financial terms, even if they cannot afford such a lifestyle. Instead of prioritizing their expenses on more important things, such as student loans, they focus on things that they can wisely do without. Dan Kadlec mentions in his article, "Millennials Are Growing Up—But They're Still Making One Huge Mistake," that *"Two in three [millennial] wants to keep pace with peers on where they live and what they wear, and the types of places they eat and the gadgets they carry."* He ends his article with, *"If they are taking their cues from peers who never miss an iPhone upgrade but have boomeranged home with Mom and Dad, they are headed in the wrong direction."* There is no originality left if one is only following wherever the trends lead them. There is nothing then that makes them themselves.

Social media does not help millennials avoid their peers' footsteps. If anything, it only perpetuates this. It is all out there in the open: if you miss a post on Facebook, it will haunt you on Instagram. You might even get a notification telling you to check your Instagram or Facebook. Twenty-five percent of millennials share online shopping content with their social networks, according to an article by Kimberlee Morrison. Then, there is the issue of electronics that keep popping up everywhere. iPhones are so absurdly expensive, yet for millennials, carrying an older version of an iPhone is like dressing up from a thrift store. Older versions of some other phones are not considered that bad, apparently, but older versions of an iPhone are. If a millennial wants to fit in among their peers, they need to upgrade their phone as soon as possible once a new one comes out. It does not matter how much it costs, because it is of the utmost priority. With every new updated phone, there is a new feature to operate social media in a 'new' and 'exciting' way that only the new phone's feature can provide. Plus, while smartphones are not as smart as they sound, they sure are sensitive. They break easily, and sometimes they stop working after just one to two years. Smartphones are also costly unless you get them on a promotion or a new sign-up with a provider. Even if a person had no intention to upgrade, they are not left with much of an option when their phone stops working altogether.

I have advised my children on this matter a vast number of times, but they do not always hear me. Once a friend tells them precisely what I said in the first place, it all suddenly makes sense to them, and they forget that I told them the exact information earlier. I realized that if I wanted to get a message through to my children, I would have to build the idea in their friends' heads to reach them. Coming from their friends, it would be far easier for them to accept and digest the message than if it was coming from me. Peer pressure and influence are normal and happen in any generation. However, in the millennials' era, it is stronger because of social media. There are just so many more ways to do it now. While there are many ways that this can be fantastic, there are just as many ways that this can be utterly disastrous.

I am always curious about what type of relationships millennials have with one another. What are the peer pressures and influences they have on each other? What are the challenges millennials face when interacting with their peers? I want to know who has the most impact on millennials, and to whom they turn in their hour of need. During my teenage years, I always went to my friends when something was bothering me. I could not open my heart and soul to my parents because the generation gap was too wide.

When I asked most millennials if they support each other as peers, the answer was always resoundingly, "*Yes!*" Natalie replied, "*Once I got into college, my friends became important to me, and I wanted to be with them constantly. Whereas in high school, I could pass by them in the hall and just say hi.*" She continued, "*Your friends become a good source for you, and you can talk to them about things you cannot bring up at home. We all come from different cultures and backgrounds, and so we hear different perspectives than what we will hear at home, which we already understand because we know how our parents and siblings think. At the same time, my friends calm me down because I am not going to go crazy in front of them and scare them off like I would with my parents.*"

However, Mike, who is from the older millennial generation, told me that millennials do not support each other as much because millennials overall lack the skills to be friends. He said, "*We all have a lot of friends on social media, but in real life, we don't have many. We have friends that we hang out with once in a while but not real friends you go to for advice or a problem. They are more people you go out with and do something different."* In essence, millennials may have a lot of people to hang out with for food or drinks and have somewhat superficial conversations with. However, they do not necessarily have a lot of people that are just willing to listen to them, have in-depth discussions, and work on problems with them.

Mike added that social media has made millennials lonely. He believes that they spend time on social media with their friends only until they feel a temporary satisfaction. He explained that even when millennials go out with friends for a social gathering, they spend their time on their phones, browsing social media platforms. He gave me an example of how once he went hiking with a group of his friends. Instead of enjoying nature, they spent virtually all their time taking photos of said nature so that they could post them on social media. They would still hike to the top of a hill, but the reason would not be so they could savor the view, but rather to take a picture of the view.

I have seen this scenario many times, but the worst is when friends or families go out to eat at a restaurant. Instead of talking with each other, each person is on their phone. I stare at them, wondering why they are at the restaurant in the first place if that is what they intend to do. What is the objective of going out together? They could have picked the food up or had it delivered to their doorstep instead of going out of their way to actually dine out. The worst is when it is a couple. I find it sad—tragic, even—that they hang out with each other but barely have anything to say.

Mike put it bluntly when he said, *"I can't imagine going to my peers if I am in a difficult situation. They are not wiser than me."* This made me wonder what judgment criteria millennials use to consider someone worthy of seeking their advice.

# CHAPTER 4

## Millennials and Social Media

*"To effectively communicate, we must realize that we are all different in the way we perceive the world and use this understanding as a guide to our communication with others."*

~ Anthony Robbins

## Evolution of Human Communications

*L*ately, it has become easier to find people on social media and get to know them than to see them in real life. The understanding of socialization has changed tremendously from the way previous generations used to socialize. Meeting in person and catching up with our life stories was something we often did during my generation. We would discuss our family, our work, and the political and economic challenges we were facing without ever running out of topics. Right up until my children were in high school, the means of socialization were standard. When social media became accessible to all, the change in communication became noticeable.

Social media has become a language in itself. To communicate quickly and briefly, millennials needed to type fast. As a result, they created a shorthand language specially designed for use over social media. For older generations, these shortcuts are still confusing. I remember when I started being active on social media and I would see people commenting with abbreviations such as LOL (laughing out loud) and BFF (best friends forever). I had to ask what they meant. I still struggle with new words or acronyms, but finally, I decided not to worry about it anymore.

Then millennials take what I have known all my life as a pound sign (#) and call it a 'hashtag.' What is ironic is that millennials believe their word is correct English and will make fun of the older generations when they still refer to it as a pound sign. I blame this on Twitter. Twitter was the first to come up with the use of hashtags in this manner, and they are now used on most social media platforms. These hashtags were designed to link users' posts to trending news stories and causes.

Language has been changing, and grammar has been evolving, since they were invented. However, the pace has considerably sped up in the past few years. I believe, with time, some of these new terms will become popular enough that various dictionaries will incorporate these new words as part of the English language.

To communicate with large audiences on social media, language abbreviations are necessary to facilitate convenience. Millennials are very crafty when it comes to using abbreviations and emojis to get their message across. This means that the older generations need to catch up and learn this evolved language form, before they stop understanding what their children and grandchildren are saying altogether.

## How Millennials Use Social Media

Social media in its present form is still relatively new, yet millennials seem to believe that they absolutely cannot live without it. Social media is potentially addictive to all generations, but to millennials, it is an essential part of their daily routine, and they must master it to perfection. The older millennial generation does not remember life before social media, and the younger millennials have never lived without it. This is because social media only became easily accessible when cell phones became smartphones and "affordable" for everyone. We rarely see a person, regardless of their age, walking without a cell phone now.

Millennials might not respond to an email for days, if not longer, but they instantly feel obligated to respond to a text message—even while driving. Although texting while driving is illegal in most states in the U.S., it is a common occurrence regardless. While one is texting, they are not alert to their environment, which any experienced driver will say is crucial to being safe on the roads. This distraction causes the driver's reaction time to substantially decrease, which makes it more likely that they will be involved in a serious accident.

The Department of Motor Vehicles (DMV) is acutely aware of the danger posed by texting while driving. They clearly state on their website, *"When you choose to text and drive, you're threatening every single driver around you—and placing more value on that text message than yourself and your fellow drivers."*

I have seen parents text and read emails while they drive. One would think adults would be more aware of the danger of such an act, but sadly, that's not the case. If parents act so irresponsibly, how can they teach their children not to behave in such a manner? This social media addiction is becoming an epidemic spreading among all generations, not just the millennials. Parents need to set a good example for the younger genera-tions—or else, we are responsible for the consequences of road accidents as much as the teens.

For millennials, the cell phone is not a device to use for phone calls anymore. It is more of a portable computer. Many millennials do not like making phone calls. They prefer text messaging and communicating through alternative social media tools. The number of applications that can be downloaded and bought on a smartphone is virtually unlimited. Social media allows people to have accessibility to other people anytime, anywhere. While most millennials use these platforms vigorously and without second thought, some do earnestly try to manage their use. Unfortunately, even if a person wishes to control their use of social media applications, it is just too difficult, since notifications continuously pop up to distract them.

Maggie is one of the millennials who became aware of how distracting social media can be and decided to control it. She told me that she spent so much time on social media that she became unproductive in her life. She missed reading books and listening to her iPod, so she turned off her notifications on the weekend to focus more on her hobbies and activities. She told me it helped her, and she became more satisfied with her accomplishments.

Only a few years ago, people were still carrying around flip phones that simply made and received calls and text messages. Today, I do not recall meeting a person with a flip phone, except my friend Lina: a young widow with two children who is barely making ends meet. She decided to stick to her old flip phone to cut down on her monthly bills, and only use her laptop to access social media. I admire her resilience to the changing status quo. However, pretty soon landline phones will disappear, just like typewriters did. Eventually, it will become difficult to find a millennial living independently with a landline. The traditional telephone is becoming useless, mainly because there are many free applications you can use to make international and local calls, such as Skype, WhatsApp, and Viber. Long-distance calls are more affordable now with cell phones, especially with the monthly plans service providers offer. Those packages sound very tempting when one can get unlimited calls and texts as part of a plan. Most millennials are still under their parents' phone plans, which makes it more affordable than if they had to purchase their own plans. Fortunately, nowadays, an adult child can move out of their parents' house, go halfway across the country, and still keep his or her old phone number on their parents' plan.

It may come as a shock to many, especially those who are not social media-savvy, to learn that all the social media forums we categorize under the same broad definition are actually vastly different. Millennials know these distinctions, and each of them has an interest in one platform over the others for various reasons. The current list of choices between social media platforms is numerous: Facebook, Instagram, Twitter, SnapChat, LinkedIn, WhatsApp, Skype, Pinterest, YouTube, and many others are all there to choose from. In terms of popularity, Facebook wins by an overwhelming margin. Today, over 1.37 billion people around the world use Facebook daily. It is the site where both family and friends are equally present.

However, it seems that over time, Facebook has lost its appeal among the youngest members of the millennial generation, who are in their teens and early twenties. They do not like using Facebook as much as other platforms; they find it better suited for the older generation, where their parents are active. As Natalie says, "*We only use Facebook to post things for our family to see and know we are alive and well. We use other social media platforms that our parents are not on so we can express ourselves freely and post anything we want.*"

The younger generation, according to Natalie, likes using Instagram and SnapChat. They love sharing photos and videos far more than they enjoy writing. They prefer to comment with emojis instead of words. What started as a small picture-video-messaging app became a way of connecting with people all over the world. They are the first generation whose every move, including mistakes and most embarrassing moments, has all been recorded, videotaped, and uploaded—perhaps for eternity.

These digital footprints will follow the millennials all of their lives. Employers and universities will check social media pages. If millennials did something stupid in high school, like getting drunk and acting foolish, footage of this will exist for decades to come. Previous generations never had to worry about their worst moments being recorded and distributed, potentially to thousands of people.

Those who knew SnapChat in its early days remember how the longest a picture or video could be seen was ten seconds, after which it would disappear forever. So, what was the point of doing something so temporary? Well, millennials found the fact that they could be connected with their friends on a daily basis, without forcing conversations over text or making time for phone calls, exceedingly appealing. They can get a quick picture sent to them, see what the other person is doing, and send something back. With this, there is a constant back and forth via pictures and videos. SnapChat is always evolving and changing to fit its consumers' needs. One of its newest features, the 'SnapMap,' allows people to post onto a collected story that people from all over the world can watch by clicking on the geographical region. This opened the app on a grand scale to not only private, but even public interactions among millennials.

I am still struggling to understand the fun of sharing a timed video for seconds. When I click to watch it and then get distracted by something else, it is gone forever by the time I get back to it. There is no replaying it once this narrow viewing period is over. I guess the saying, "*A picture is worth a thousand words*" really applies to this new style of communication. On the other hand, by having these conversations disappear, millennials are protected in case they have said or shared anything that they don't want to be memorialized forever.

Social media has expanded to engaging people professionally and educationally, not just socially. There are many useful educational apps on social media that millennials follow. The intense competition in the industry compels companies to make their services more interesting for their users. As a result, they end up producing things that are hugely well-received by millennial audiences. On the professional level, LinkedIn is an excellent platform that allows professionals to network with other professionals and find new opportunities. Also, one can find a large number of articles that are relevant to their field of education and work. LinkedIn also tells its members about conferences and other professional events going on in their area.

A few of the millennials I interviewed told me how active they are on LinkedIn. Tarek connected with companies that he was interested in working for by searching individuals who worked there on LinkedIn and connecting with them. As a result, he scheduled an in-person meeting with an employee, who shared information on the company and how he should apply for a job there. Other times, Tarek reached out directly to the founders and CEOs of the organizations he was interested in working for, messaging them through LinkedIn to express his interest and tell them why he thought he was a good fit for their companies. One of these founders met with him and explained that at the time, they did not have openings, but he was interested in Tarek's resume for the future.

If millennials utilize LinkedIn in a positive way, it is a useful platform to network and find jobs. It is also an excellent place to get a sense of what companies are out there relevant to the types of situation and working experience millennial job-seekers are looking for. Creating an account on LinkedIn is a must to be able to network and apply for good jobs. There are even professionals who provide the service of creating a personalized LinkedIn profile, because it is so important to have an impressive profile. Many companies look people up on their LinkedIn profile when they apply for a job as an initial review of the person. Some Human Resource personnel and recruiting agencies reach out to individuals on LinkedIn to invite them to apply for jobs that are suitable to their experience and relevant to that company's requirements. Also, individuals can ask people in their LinkedIn networks whom they have worked with in the past to endorse specific skills highlighted in their profiles and write recommendations that could make their profile look good.

Thus, some social media platforms are educational and can be used in a good way. I am also thoroughly impressed by how many millennials enjoy using these platforms to learn about various topics. YouTube and Podcast are examples of educational applications through which millennials gain knowledge by watching videos or listening to audios. Virtually every possible topic of discussion is covered by these platforms. That does not mean they cannot be used negatively, but the fact that they are educational is a massive advantage—especially from my point of view as a parent.

I learned about Podcasts a year ago from my son. I have enjoyed listening to topics related to millennials, business, and positive thinking. While I am driving, I listen to a number of Podcast audios, and I do not get as frustrated being stuck in D.C. traffic as I used to. Sandy, for example, told me she is very interested in health and fitness. She watches YouTube videos that discuss fitness and exercises. She also listens to inspirational topics on Podcast while she is exercising.

Makeup tutorials on YouTube and Instagram are also very popular. Natalie learned how to do her own makeup by watching YouTube videos; she became so good at it that during prom, she did her friends' makeup as well. The following year, many girls from her high school paid her to do their makeup. She ended up doing a great job and even made a few bucks along the way.

Social media can be called a form of culture and fashion on its own. The younger generation of millennials likes posting "memes," especially about funny things. Maybe it is a way to deal with stress, or perhaps it is just a different kind of humor, but it does seem to always lift their mood even about the most depressing things. Livewires defines memes as "*Captioned photos that are intended to be funny, often as a way to publicly ridicule human behavior. Other memes can be videos and verbal expressions. Some memes have heavier and more philosophical content.*"

Natalie says, "*We are a happy generation because we can find the fun in the bad.*" She added that social media is their ultimate comfort. "*We know so much about what is going on around the world through social media and to deal with all the awful things happening, we laugh through memes. It is an escape from reality and our comfort zone.*"

Social media has also developed into a shopping platform for millennials. Most online businesses nowadays are created and designed by millennials, according to the U.S. Chamber of Commerce Foundation. As a result, it comes as no surprise that they use platforms such as Facebook and Instagram to market and promote their products. Sometimes, when I am watching my children on social media using artistic apps, they look like complete pros—almost as if they were born to work on these apps.

The speed with which their fingers glide over the screen and the rate at which their minds comprehend the absurdly complex interface makes me feel as if I have time traveled from the past into the future. I continue to be shocked by the endless advances in technology. I try to learn from them, so I can master the use of these apps and remain up-to-date as well—but whenever I do, I realize that it is not my passion.

I have, however, made myself useful by sharing some ideas with my children regarding their online business. Dena is very artistic. She decided to design her own range of products, such as mugs, t-shirts, and hats, and sell them online. Through this business, Dena was able to accomplish many of her dreams. She utilized her art skills, applied what she learned in marketing, and became more knowledgeable about online marketing while she was generating income from her business.

I never realized there were so many online stores that marketed themselves through Facebook and Instagram. I started following some of these businesses and noticed that some of their founders were younger than twenty-one years old. This generation is remarkably entrepreneurial and innovative. They want to become successful by working independently. Some establish these businesses while studying in college or set them up as an additional means of generating income while working a full-time job.

This generation is distinct from all past generations. Each day, an innovation enters the market, or a new idea becomes a trend. Millennials know how to continually stay up-to-date and adopt new things seamlessly. Their out-of-the-box approach lets them take these innovations to the next level within days. That is called value addition, which has been performed by previous generations, but never on this scale. I love this aspect of social media.

Millennial consumers are also actively engaged in online businesses by expressing their honest opinion about their products. Sometimes, they can be hurtful with their comments, but they are nevertheless giving their feedback. Of course, there is a downside for having so many marketing platforms, which is why millennials find themselves shopping for items that they may not even need. Yet, they buy them nevertheless because they are trending. I have noticed through these online businesses that millennials are now the largest shopping demographic. I am still a shopper at Amazon, but even I have started feeling that shopping via Amazon will eventually become old-fashioned next to the latest online business trends.

Millennials understand how to tactfully use each social media platform for their benefit. Some of them are even 'Insta-famous' from simply posting attractive pictures of themselves while advertising products, ranging from fashion and beauty products to services and restaurants. They use this fame for business and marketing opportunities. For example, a popular 'Insta-famous' model can advertise a teeth whitening kit by posting a beautiful, high-quality picture of herself using it and showing her perfect teeth. The products are usually sponsored by the company that wants to sell the product, and the Instagram models typically announce this to their followers as part of the marketing approach. Through this process, millennials can target other millennials in an app that is already millennial-dominant. The opportunities are numerous and lucrative.

Millennials are mostly unreceptive to traditional methods of advertising; because of this, marketing executives have to come up with entirely new methods of selling products to this demographic. But by exploiting the power of social media, companies can create positive word-of-mouth among their target audience, which is smart.

Twitter is an interesting platform in that most of its users belong to the eighteen to twenty-four-year-old age group. However, many of the millennials I interviewed were not keen on Twitter. They did not find it user-friendly and preferred other mediums. Twitter is, in many ways, similar to Facebook, in the sense that you can make posts with texts, pictures, or videos. The key difference is that you are limited to a maximum of 280 characters per tweet. In a statistical analysis done by Digital Dealer, 61 percent of all Twitter users are millennials. Twitter is one of those things that you either love or hate. It can be complex in its structure and tends to be brimming with pointless memes and funny posts that many might not understand or be interested in. Nonprofit organizations use it quite often to tweet about their work or events of relevance happening around the world. Many celebrities also first opt for a Twitter account rather than a Facebook or Instagram account, as their followers know that anything posted from a verified account on Twitter is authentic. Yet at the same time, Twitter is notorious for being one of the key breeding grounds for hateful Internet trolls and cyberbullying, which are a severe problem on certain platforms.

Social media connects people from all over the globe. Mike has family living abroad, and through Facebook, he knows that they are doing well. He also gets a chance to share the beautiful poems he writes about social justice. He told me, "*I like having a say and being able to contribute to issues of the world by posting poems and my opinion on Facebook.*" He feels that without Facebook, he would not know what is going on around the world, or even in his home country. Mike also appreciates that he gets to learn from his friends' and family's posts what mainstream news does not cover. Posts from his friends offer a different insight into issues he cares about and give him an original view.

Maggie's family lives in a different state, and therefore she does not get to see them often. Her brother frequently travels abroad on missions, and she enjoys watching his posts and photos on Facebook. She also enjoys seeing pictures of her nephew, who is now six years old. Maggie remarked, "*It is a nice way to see family regularly when you cannot be with them.*" These two are not alone in this sentiment. Hundreds of millions of people around the world are deeply grateful for this feature provided by social media. Even the elderly desperately try to learn how to use social media platforms so that they can stay updated continuously with their children's activities when they are living far from them.

I recall recently I was traveling to the Middle East for business and I visited an old friend. We sat and talked as if we had never been never apart. Then she asked me how I was finding the country and her family. I thought that I would be surprised because I had not seen the place or her family for more than six years. But in reality, I felt as if I had seen them not long ago. Then we both realized that we saw each other daily through social media and felt caught up. Before social media was invented, I used to get excited to see old friends and hear all about what I had missed. Now, we can be anywhere in the world in our minds as if we are there physically.

No matter what age one is, if a person is active on social media, he or she will see much of what is happening around the world through their newsfeeds. Many Millennials get their news from social media—Facebook and Twitter specifically. Information coming directly from the President of the United States (POTUS) is often seen on Twitter before any of the news channels can make a segment about it. Millennials form increasingly complex views as they are exposed to like-minded individuals, for better or worse. Either way, compared to other generations, many millennials have broken the stigma of having the same views as their parents. They are attuned to the digital era. As a result, they have learned to figure things out on their own. It is this vast bank of information that cultivates beliefs and views, not what societal hegemony teaches them.

I enjoy reading exciting posts shared on social media. While I was writing this book, many articles and videos about millennials started popping up that I found very useful. Social media plays a good role in bringing justice and equality to those who need it. For example, when a natural disaster takes place, one hears about it first thing on social media.

On several occasions, I have woken up to find that something horrifying has occurred somewhere—not because of the news, but because one of my Facebook friends marked themselves as safe during an incident or natural disaster. If any injustice takes place in a country, such as the Syrian refugee crisis, social media exposes it and covers it far better than the actual news media.

I appreciate the rising awareness about these affairs among millennials, all thanks to social media. What I like even more is the fact that millennials actively participate in efforts to raise awareness about these issues. They have developed a greater understanding of what is going on around the world than the previous generation, due to their transcontinental relationship with social media.

Lastly, social media can be a form of stress release. Many millennials tend to express their mental state through social media, which can be a helpful valve to release any pent-up stress in a way that is not harmful. People's positive comments and encouragement can be vital in making a person feel that he or she is not alone. Natalie said, "*We support each other when we realize that one of our friends or peers is sharing something sad, and we tend to call or chat in support.*" Social media can provide emotional support to anyone, and particularly to those who are housebound, having an emotional crisis, or just prefer to chat about their problems online rather than in person. Twenty-four hours a day, seven days a week, 365 days a year, there is somebody willing to listen online.

## What Millennials Dislike About Social Media

Strangely enough, millennials do have issues with social media, even though they are utterly addicted to it. The large number of social media platforms, along with regular apps, can become overwhelming to manage at times. Instead of becoming a stress reliever, they can instead become a source of stress. When I asked millennials if there is anything they do not like about social media, I did not expect to hear so many criticisms of it. Most millennials I interviewed expressed that they have experienced distress and anxiety from their social media activities.

It seems Facebook stresses millennials the most. On Facebook, people post their opinions, travel photos, news about their newborn babies, wedding photos, and more. This may appear as if they are boasting and showing off their lives' blessings. I was told that those postings, in general, do not represent the real lives that millennials are living. Instead, they are an artificial projection that millennials want to showcase to their friends and family: one that screams that they are pleased and successful. This is sad because it forces some millennials to take numerous photos of themselves in all kinds of poses and positions before they are satisfied with one picture to upload. And instead of enjoying the moment, many young people who are out swimming, skiing, or at a concert are thinking about how they will look in their Instagram photo, instead of how much fun they are having at the event.

Most millennials I interviewed said that their friends post photos and quips that make their lives look glamorous and desirable. Some even admitted to doing this themselves. Maggie explains this behavior by saying, *"I assume it is difficult for a person to post on social media about their problems or depressing life. However, there is no need to post otherwise unless it makes them believe their own lie."* She further elaborated, *"People don't post bad stuff like my husband is a jerk, or my mom is being crazy. You only see the good on social media."* She believes that social media can become a narcissistic tool where people endlessly show off and brag.

Mona says people that post the most are either unhappy or trying to convey certain things. In some cases, they just want to show off their affluent lifestyle. She said that whenever she talks to them in person, she hears something different than what they post online. They incessantly complain about issues in their life. This negativity is a far cry from the positive posts they have embellished all over their social media profiles.

Mona said what people post is often a 'phormo' (a person continually texting or talking on the phone when at a party, club, bar, or any other social event). She said that when my generation went to college, we knew what each one of us was doing and how he or she was feeling. After college, people spread out, and the only thing we know about them now comes from social media. Due to this, it is hard to tell if their posts are genuine and sincere anymore. People tend to brag more when no one knows what exactly they are doing or not doing.

Mona also believes that social media can make a person depressed. She told me that when she sees posts of her friends out socializing and she is not invited, she finds herself lonely and sad. This sensation is so prevalent, in fact, that it even has its own Internet abbreviation: FOMO, or 'fear of missing out.'

Of course, it stands to reason that the more hours a day somebody spends online, the more likely it is that they are depressed. They are spending all their time on the phone or their computer, when they could be spending their time more productively learning a hobby, reading, studying a new language, or spending time with people off-line.

Sandy, twenty-six, expressed something very interesting about social media, specifically Facebook. She said, "Social media is great in the way that it connects people, but also it can be isolating if you are not in the right state of mind. It can make you feel lonely." She also added, "*Everything on social media seems like a perfect projection of what they want people to see. It gets difficult when you see that over and over again, and you find yourself questioning: should I be doing this now?*" Sandy said that when she is on Facebook and watching her friends' and peers' posts, she starts evaluating and questioning her own life. She said, "*I start doubting myself.*" It's truly sad that social media can have such an effect on a person.

Ola shared similar feelings as Sandy when she told me that she closed all of her social media accounts; she was getting depressed seeing people posting about their newborn babies when she was having difficulty conceiving a baby. She told me that she felt jealous of how happy and accomplished they seemed, when she was not. I was shocked to hear her say that, because she is married to someone whom she loves dearly and who seems like a lovely person.

I believe that social media is isolating millennials socially. They are satisfied with communicating with friends and family members through social media, but they do not see any use or reason in calling or meeting people in person. I did not grow up on social media, so it is easier for me to limit my use and access to it than for a millennial to do the same. Moreover, I honestly believe that having a relationship in person helps me judge if what I see on social media is genuinely true or exaggerated. I find myself feeling sorry for people who post every detail of their lives as if they are trying to convince themselves of their happiness. If one is truly happy, they do not need to let the world know about it; they know they are content, and that is all that matters.

Sandy put it beautifully when she said that it took her a while to figure it out, but she eventually realized that the exaggerated postings were, rather tragically, nothing but a sign of insecurity. She said, "*People that I know do not have a great relationship always post how happy they are in their relationship. It's as if they are trying to project to everybody how great their relationship is when, in reality, it is not.*"

Maggie commented, "*I think people can get mixed up by spending so much time on social media and learning what their friends and others are doing to a point where they feel they had enough socialization. However, millennials that are hooked on social media can end up losing their in-person social and network skills.*" Maggie also confirmed that social media can never replace having an in-person friendship.

Millennials tend to become sensitive on social media and take things extra personally. This reaction adds to their stress and affects their relationship with their friends and family. Natalie told me, "*I see people stressing out about posting the perfect photo.*" Many millennials care about the photos they post online. They want to look nothing less than perfect, and they are willing to retake selfies endlessly until they find the ideal photo to share. Looking at their selfies often makes millennials stress out about the way they look, even if there is absolutely nothing wrong with the picture or their looks. This can cause problems, such as body dysmorphia or eating disorders, among both girls and boys, although girls tend to be more adversely affected.

I witnessed this preoccupation with appearance with one of my daughters, who is never satisfied with her photo. Of course, the worst pictures of her are the ones that I take. I might not be good at taking photos, but I do find her photos pretty, unlike she does. It is an emotional side of her that she apparently does not want anyone in the world, besides herself, to see. She always comes up with something wrong in these pictures. The flaw can be so utterly minimal that no normal person would ever notice it unless they were closely scrutinizing the photo or looking for that specific blemish. I love natural images where I do not have to pose. In fact, I miss seeing natural photos of people in action rather than posing perfectly for a photo. Images on social media are mostly selfies, which are often all about how stunning one looks.

With the development of smartphones, millennials instantly invented selfies. They are very conscious about their appearances, through no fault of their own, because this is what online culture has morphed into. Despite this, many still enjoy sharing their pictures with their friends. Taking a selfie from a phone has become so easy and common that even toddlers are capable of it. Millennials even know how to filter the photo to make themselves look thinner or their skin look clearer. I recall there was a period when millennials posted "duck face" photos. I do not know how to express it clearly in words, but it went something along the lines of this: the person would pose with their lips pursed tight and sticking outwards. I thought it was weird, but then I saw my kids and their friends obsessed by posting pictures with this pose until this trend eventually died down. I hated looking at photos of my children's faces looking so bizarre. I could not, for the life of me, understand why they would turn their beauty into something ugly and fake.

The older members of the millennial generation also seem to miss the way photos used to be taken. Maggie told me that she is not a fan of how taking pictures for the sake of memory has started to gradually vanish, and taking selfies has become the thing.

Another issue millennials suffer from on social media is: "*Why didn't a lot of people like my post?*" On Facebook and Instagram, people post photos and posts. The person who posted can see who liked it and who commented. People find themselves tallying how many people responded: who liked their post, and who did not react among their friends and family. Some people post so often that it gets hard to keep up.

Occasionally, I might like a post because I happened to see it and its message was to my taste. At the same time, I might miss numerous other posts only because I am not checking my social media accounts every single minute. However, I also do not get lots of likes on some of my posts. I assume this is because I am not very active on social media. I know so many people who can catch up with every single post on every single social media platform, even though they have full-time jobs and families to care for. I honestly wonder when they have the time to do all this. This has made me realize that it is indeed a skill to be active on social media and simultaneously fulfill your life's responsibilities. I, for one, am not able to do it.

Another form of stress millennials put themselves through is when a friend unfollows or unfriends them on social media. There is a button that you can click to unfollow someone you had agreed to follow at one point. It is handy. I have used it to unfollow certain people when they posted radical things on my Facebook timeline. I not only disagreed with their views, but also I did not want to be associated with their ideologies in any way, shape, or form—and that includes social media. Some posts make bigoted, racist, or partisan comments about other's beliefs. I do not like to play party to any of this. At other times, I unfollow people who post too frequently. It is irritating to open a social application and be bombarded by endless posts by the same person. Indeed, everyone knows that one person who attends several social events and then posts multiple, mostly indistinguishable, photos and selfies at every event. (I would never know what the event was, because a selfie does not tell very much about it.) Every time I scroll through my newsfeed, I would find one person's face plastered all over it. So, BAM! I unfollowed them.

Some millennials spend too much time being upset and trying to figure out why a person has unfollowed them. Their response is to stop communicating with that person altogether.

Quite a few millennials have told me that Facebook is carefully tailored. People want you to exclusively agree with and believe in their point of view. They try to manipulatively condition you with their way of thinking. This was clear during the U.S. presidential election in 2016, when people were expressing their views against Donald Trump or Hillary Clinton bluntly and with frustration. I know some situations in which friends completely stopped talking to each other because they stood on opposite sides of the political aisle.

People were very engaged on social media during the elections, but not necessarily in a positive way. Instead, these interactions were often conducted in an angry way. The toxicity was so extreme that I think we lost the essence of our democracy during that recent election by not being respectful of how each person expresses different opinions on social media. People reached a point where they would block or unfollow each other if they felt slightly offended by their friends' counter opinions. People ended up losing friends who were good in every other way, but had differing views about politics.

Moreover, people often say things online that they would never say to someone's face—like calling them a name or swearing at them. This is particularly true in forums that allow people to post anonymously.

Social media, like every other culture, has its pros and cons. Before the invention of digital social media, people had more of a private life; a person would usually confide in and share personal information with close friends and family members. Nowadays, millennials are too transparent about their lives and are open to publicly sharing their daily whereabouts, stories, and incidents. This can be seen as a good thing because it makes this generation more confident and less finicky. However, there is another way to look at it: why overshare at all? I am not sure how interested people are in where or what another person ate today. I have seen young people post things on social media when they are drunk, and, the next day, wish the ground underneath them would open and swallow them.

Mike is cautious in his use of social media. He does not believe in sharing personal information publicly because, as he put it, "*It can bite us back.*" He said that due to his military background and training, "*I can write a profile about a person based on how much they post about their life: where they eat, travel, who they meet and where they meet.*" Mike believes that people should be careful on social media and avoid oversharing. With the amount of information people give out in their profiles and accounts, it is not difficult to build a detailed database about a person's likes, dislikes, locations, places visited, eating habits, workplaces, and so on. One can come up with a list of areas likely to be visited by a person based on their preferences; it is even possible to gauge what time they might have gone there and what possible routes they might have taken. Any such data can be used against an individual.

Everyone would be well advised to think twice before posting, particularly if slightly impaired by alcohol or fatigue. Some of these posts can follow millennials all of their lives. Even if they delete them the next day, somebody may have already made a copy, forwarded, or retweeted the original post.

Millennials should also be careful about how they phrase things on social media because they can be misconstrued. Some things they say can sound hostile in print, which would not have seemed that way in person, where there is ample time and opportunity for clarification. Debate and different opinions are healthy and constructive, but ad hominem attacks online can never be justified. One might not even know that person in real life, so it's not worth getting upset about what a stranger posted.

# Millennials and Video Games

Although video games are different from social media, they both involve using a computer or a smartphone. Unfortunately, video gaming can become an addiction. With today's accessibility to online services, millennials have more games to play, and for longer hours. Keith Bakker, Director of Smith & Jones Addiction Consultants, tells WebMD he created the new program in response to a growing problem among young men and boys. "The more we looked at it, the more we saw [gaming] was taking over the lives of kids."

Kimberly Young, PsyD, clinical director of the Center for Internet Addiction and author of *Caught in the Net*, says that compulsive gaming meets addiction criteria; she has seen severe withdrawal symptoms in game addicts. She says, "*They become angry, violent, or depressed. If [parents] take away the computer, their child sits in the corner and cries, refuses to eat, sleep, or do anything.*"

Sometimes, parents are tired from running after their children all day and want to distract them by putting on a game for them to play. They are relieved for a while seeing their children being entertained and occupied. It allows them to catch up with work or other things, without realizing the amount of time their children are spending on games—until it starts getting out of hand.

Let me share a story of a dear friend of mine who has a twelve year-old child addicted to video games. Laura lost her husband to cancer a year ago, when her son Mike was eleven. She was devastated about losing her husband and became very concerned about how she would take care of her family, financially and emotionally. Mike used to play video games on and off, but after the passing of his father, he started playing games regularly. I went to visit them a year after her husband's passing and stayed at their house for a week. Throughout that time, I didn't see Mike during the evening or late at night. I only saw him at 5:00 AM when I woke up from my jetlag and he was playing games. I asked him if he just woke up, and he responded, while moving the remote in his hands so fast, fixated by the screen of the TV, by saying, "*No. I haven't slept yet.*" I looked at the time and asked him when he planned on sleeping, and he casually responded, "*Whenever I get tired.*" This went on for the entire week I was there.

When I spoke with Laura about it, she expressed concern, but didn't know what to do. She seemed to believe that she had already talked to him enough about this issue and there was nothing else she could do about it. I suggested to her: "Why not take the remote with you to work? That way, he will not be able to play until you get home." She was not a strong disciplinarian and appeared to be too reluctant to upset her son by setting rules for him. A year later, I visited them; to my astonishment, everything was exactly the same.

That doesn't mean there is no solution for such a habit. According to PsychGuides.com, "Video game addiction can be just as dangerous as any other addiction and should be treated as such. The first step in overcoming dependency is being able to recognize that it exists." The article goes on to provide other solutions, such as cognitive behavioral therapy, that help a person regain self-control from addiction. "The addict will undergo a series of steps to change gaming behaviors and perceptions about the relevance of video games. If the addiction is the result of another underlying problem, therapy can also address this other issue and teach the addict how to cope with conditions such as depression, stress, and anxiety."

I think at a young age, it is helpful to distract children with other interests that are useful and enable them to further develop their personalities. Doing more outdoor activities can break the routine of sitting all day playing games, and it's healthy for the kids. I suggested that my friend Laura put her son in a summer camp or take him for evening walks. I even told her that maybe she should give him house chores; that way, he would become distracted a bit.

Instead Mike's sedentary lifestyle and game addiction may have led to his obesity; his obesity led to his classmates' bullying and making fun of him in school. This increased Mike's addiction by making him not want to socialize with anyone except virtual friends.

The concern of addiction to games, in general, is an issue, but parents should be particularly worried when their children are addicted to violent games, or when they lose grasp of reality and begin to think that the game is part of life. They might snap easily at others or behave erratically.

Video games are not necessarily bad, as long as they are controlled. Dr. Shawn Green from the University of Rochester conducted a study that showed benefits from video games. "Action video games are fast-paced, and there are peripheral images and events popping up, and disappearing. These video games are teaching people to become better at taking sensory data in, and translating it into correct decisions."

Jane McGonigal, a game designer and author, says, "We have a real sense of optimism in our abilities and our opportunities to get better and succeed, and more physical and mental energy to engage with difficult problems."

Moderation in everything is best. Parents need to supervise their children while playing video games, monitor the type of games they play, and limit the number of hours that children play every day.

# CHAPTER 5

## Heading to College

*"Educating the mind without educating the heart is no education at all."*

~ Aristotle

*M*illennials are better educated than any other generation. There is a noticeable influx in the number of educated millennials especially in those who are getting their master's degree. Four in ten millennial workers aged twenty-five to twenty-nine had at least a bachelor's degree in 2016, according to a Pew Research Center analysis of Current Population Survey data. College attainment for millennial women has also improved. In 2014, statistics showed that 27 percent of millennial women have at least a bachelor's degree whereas only 7 percent of Silent Generation females (aged eighteen to thirty-three) had completed a bachelor's degree. An approximate 21 percent of millennial men have at least a bachelor's degree, while only 12 percent of Silent Generation men have a bachelor's degree.

Advancement in technology is one factor that has contributed to the high numbers of millennials who have attained academic degrees. The Internet has made the millennials curious and willing to discover knowledge; with the easy dispensation of information now, it is much easier for them to satisfy that curiosity. It also helps them not to look at the educational system with the traditional mind-set of their parents since the educational systems have also kept pace with technology.

I remember during my youth, we would sing the famous song "Another Brick in the Wall," by Pink Floyd, as an anthem. The song starts out saying,

"We don't need no education." (Yes, the double negative was deliberate!) This originated as a protest against rigid schooling, boarding schools—especially in the UK—and the idea that schools were teaching vulnerable kids propaganda and exercising "thought control." According to *Wikipedia*, this song alone from the album *The Wall*, sold over four million copies worldwide.

I used to think that education was something negative when I listened to the song, but as I grew older, I started realizing the importance of education and the doors it opens. Millennials now are more aware of this fact. Due to technological developments, they have more unconventional major options than during my generation, when most people studied to be doctors, engineers, lawyers, or other well-known professions. Millennials can study anything from social media management, blogging, robotic engineering, game design, to e-commerce. It is possible to find university programs that are tailored to what a person wants to study, rather than following mainstream programs. Students today do not even need to physically go to college to earn a degree. They can study online and complete virtual programs. Many millennials want to be their own bosses: partly because they saw that the boomers did not protect the economy, resulting in the Great Recession of 2007-2009. The boomers also allowed the national debt to skyrocket, and they do not all have ample savings for retirement. Millennials have learned from their parents' mistakes.

Although the educational system has improved since the '70s and '80s, it is still behind. The curriculum needs modifications to catch up. Linda Nilson shows in her book, *Teaching at Its Best*, that millennials receive weaker K-12 education in public schools than previous generations. This has not stopped millennials from flooding into colleges and getting an education. Nilson also mentions in her book that "*[Millennials] combined family and school experience, along with their heavy mass media exposure, [has] made them self-confident, extremely social, technologically sophisticated, action bent, goal oriented, service or civic minded, and accustomed to functioning as part of a team.*"

Schools need to develop their educational systems and curricula to prepare children for college better. This needs to start with elementary education for the upcoming generation. I predict that, in a few years, more people will be doing their education online; not only will they save on tuition, which is much cheaper online, but also it is more flexible. People can study online while maintaining full-time jobs; they can plan their studying according to their work schedule. Many can study and work right from their desks at home using Skype, FaceTime, email, and cellphones, punctuated by the occasional in-person meeting.

## The Role High Schools Play

In high schools, counselors play an important role in preparing students for college. Students need advice on what courses and how many credits they need to take to graduate and get into college. They also seek advice on how to apply for colleges, how to apply for financial aid and scholarships, how to choose which universities are most appropriate for their studies of interest, and what path they should take to get where they want to be. The question is: are all students aware of the role counselors play? Do students meet with counselors in high school regularly and seek proper guidance? How qualified and knowledgeable are counselors in high schools?

A survey conducted in 2015 by Youth Truth, a San Francisco-based nonprofit, examined the responses of 165,000 high school students and found that 44.8 percent of students feel positive about their college and career readiness. The survey also indicated that students were more likely to agree that their school helped them prepare for college than that their school helped them prepare for the careers they want. Students were also asked whether they used their schools' support services to help them achieve their future goals. Here are some of those results.

- 42 percent used college entrance exam preparation services.
- 36 percent used counseling for help with future career possibilities.
- 34 percent used counseling for help with college admissions requirements.
- 32 percent used counseling for help with applying for college.
- 23 percent used counseling for help with paying for college.

In November 2014, the White House convened a summit on strengthening the role of counseling and college advising, particularly focusing on underserved student populations. Experts emphasized that "...*counselors need to know more about the college process than their own experiences and to have the tools to be able to reach out to high school students who traditionally may not have thought about higher education as an option.*"

About forty of the country's 400-plus school counseling programs have graduate courses in college counseling, offered in degree, certificate, and continuing education programs, according to the National Association for College Admission Counseling and the American School Counselor Association. Every state has its own licensing criteria, so credentials of counselors vary from state to state.

The 2016 report by Ed Trust, "*Meandering toward Graduation: Transcript Outcomes of High School Graduates*," shows that 47 percent of students who graduate from American high schools do not complete college. Those who did graduate from high school went into the job market without a clear path or specific objective. This research has made both educators and policymakers more aware of the need for sharper focus on college and career readiness. High schools are giving priority to the credits needed for graduation over the knowledge and skills development that prepare students for life after graduation.

I did not play a significant role in my children's high school lives, especially in their senior year. I did not understand the system well enough to be able to guide my children on what courses they should take to graduate with relevance to what they wanted to do. I had also forgotten the details of the college application process; it seemed that I had graduated a hundred years ago. Many things had changed since my time, when it was much less difficult to get into a good college—not to mention, much less expensive. Everything from the application portal to the requirements had become foreign.

When I was about to graduate from high school, I knew my only choice was Colorado University, in Boulder, where we lived at that time. All my siblings went there, and I wanted to go there too. My parents played zero role in the process; I did everything on my own except my father paid the tuition, for which I was very grateful. So when it came to my children applying for college, I did not think I should play a role unless they asked me. I assumed this was the role of the school and counselors. My purpose was to make sure my children understood that they needed to study and get an excellent G.P.A. to go to college. I had lengthy discussions with my children about what they wanted to major in and which universities around us were good for that major, and encouraged them to apply for colleges early on.

Natalie visited the counselor at her high school often, and I felt she knew what she was doing. I had to travel for a family emergency during Natalie's senior year in high school; I was gone for about two months. I would call Natalie often and check on her, but we never went into detail about her college applications. She asked me one time how she would pay for the application fees, and I told her to use my credit card. I thought things were going well on the university application front. I had no worries. When I returned home, I learned that Natalie had applied to just two universities: Virginia Tech (VT) and James Madison University (JMU). She was interested in going to VT because her brother went there and it is a good school. She did not expend effort to apply for more options, in case she was not accepted by either school. Eventually, I convinced her to apply for George Mason University, which was close to home and would save me dorm fees and transportation costs.

Natalie is an independent and responsible child. In high school, she visited the counselor regularly to prepare for college. I was surprised to learn that the counselor did not work with Natalie on the details that I thought were important. One of the things we learned while waiting to hear back from the colleges that Natalie applied to was that it is better to declare a major on the applications than to put "undecided." Universities usually look at the declared majors as one of the criteria; if a student's major is not declared, their application can be pushed for further review based on availability after all the students for that calendar year are accepted. Natalie did not declare her major when she submitted the two applications because she was unsure of what she wanted to major in at the time.

The counselor should have worked with Natalie on this, or at least given her a little direction to think about what she wanted to do. If she had known this would affect her acceptance, I'm sure she would have listed a major that could have been a potential option. Once she figured out what she wanted to major in, she could have changed it. Natalie did not get accepted at VT until the third cycle, which was too long for her to wait. She got nervous that if she did not accept the offers from JMU and George Mason, she might lose those opportunities. She accepted the JMU option. About a month afterward, she received a note from VT that she had been accepted.

There were no regrets about not getting into VT in time because JMU was stronger in nursing than VT, which Natalie decided on as a major. When I tried to understand from Natalie what kind of support the counselor provided her, I realized it was information that any person could find online:

how to apply for college. Whether a student learns about the process through a high school counselor or looks it up online, the outcome might not be much different. Eventually, students must do further research on their own.

A number of millennials, ranging from the ones I interviewed to the ones I know, told me that they didn't visit the counselor's office, or they did most of the research on their own. Mona told me she did not know what she wanted to study in college, but she went ahead and declared marketing as her major on her application, just because she wanted to get accepted to VT. She told me, "*I could always change my major once I'm in, but I knew that if I declare a major, I would have a better chance to get accepted.*" She was accepted at VT in the first round. She never had to change her major; it grew on her with time. Natalie believes that counselors in high school are helpful to some extent, but students and parents do additional research on the college process.

Some parents take their children to visit universities during their late junior or early senior years; some even travel to other states. On the other hand, some students do everything themselves. Whatever the case is, I think this is an excellent way to provide students with a hands-on experience with the campus environment; however, it is not always practical or feasible for all parents.

Natalie also explained how during senior year, counselors met with students a few times per semester to go through the college application process and discuss majors that meet the students' interests. They also provided relevant information about colleges that offer those majors. She did, however, emphasize that you had to approach counselors if you needed support; most of her friends did not meet with counselors, and tried to figure their way on their own. When I tried to understand from Natalie how counselors guided students, she said: "*They basically link you to resources that are out there, and you can research on your own.*"

Another way students learn about the college application process is through high school visits, where college students hold meetings with high school seniors to talk about what is out there. The college students provide high school students with necessary information about the college they are representing, as well as the application process.

Some students did not feel their high school counselor understood how to guide them. Sandy said, "*My counselor in high school tried to push me to go to colleges that didn't make sense for what I wanted to do. Counselors are not specialized in everyone's focused area, and it is hard for them to be able to guide all students. If you are a motivated person like me, counselors can help you so much."*

I think Sandy raises a good point. There need to be specialized counselors or advisors who can guide the students who are more focused on what they want to study, not just general guidance that applies to all.

Most parents play an essential role in their children's education; they understand their children's interests better than a counselor. Of course, this is not meant to undermine the role of school counselors, because I believe they are capable of guiding students who are going toward general majors, or who do need direction. But the school system needs to advance to keep up with new majors arising as a result of technology.

It is not enough for counselors to just provide the students with general information that can be researched easily. The education sector needs to invest in educating and training counselors regularly, so that they can be of better guidance to the next generations. Sandy believes that parents' advice on education makes a huge difference. She gave the example of her boyfriend, whose mother had a different parenting style and was hands-off in his decisions. He struggled in college and dropped out because he could not figure out what he wanted to study, or how to go about paying his financial payments and loans. There are many students who want to go to college, but do not have the support—especially financial support. Some do not wish to carry a load of student loans; however, I am sure there are other ways to go about it if some guidance is provided.

For example, when I was struggling as a single mother to put my son through university, I asked him to go to community college for two years and work part-time to save some money. In addition, I asked him to look into scholarships that could help. When I tried to look into scholarships for my children, I was overwhelmed by the options and the competition. I asked the university advisor for support, but all I received were endless links to scholarships that required a full-time job just to apply, in the hope that we would get something. Similarly, the Free Application for Financial Student Aid (FAFSA) was something I dreaded each semester. It never got any easier, no matter how often I filled out the application; there were always glitches on the website. But I put up with it each year because I needed the support.

One of the things I learned while writing this book is that online surveys exist that match people to the areas they are best at. They are not specific; for example, the survey might tell the person that they are good in science, math, or literature, but it does not go into greater depth (e.g., if the person is better suited to biology or mechanical engineering). But the downfall is that students do not necessarily understand themselves well at that stage, and might not get the correct results. Also, the survey results do not always match people in the right fields.

For example, I completed some of those surveys myself to understand how they work. One of the results that gave me pause was, "I enjoy working with people, and I have strong verbal and written communication skills." Hmmm! I am not sure I had those skills at the age of eighteen. Even if I did, I'm not certain that I would have wanted to pursue a career based on that criterion. These are skills that a person acquires with experience, but are not essential to decide on a major. Another question that made me frustrated: "I'm interested in intellectual ideas, including those that are shaped by religious beliefs." I am interested in intellectual ideas, but what do religious beliefs have to do with it? So what do I choose in this case—yes or no? I am half-interested. If I choose yes, I might end up being guided to theology. I am not necessarily saying it is wrong to do self-tests and surveys online, but they might only guide one to general interests, but not what one would like to be for the rest of their life.

The majority of the millennials I interviewed, including my children, took the self-tests but did not feel they led them to understand their passion for a particular major. Tarek ended up studying math because he likes numbers. He hates math but likes engineering.

I don't think parents should play a huge role in their children's decision of what to study in college. Parents can play a supportive role, and if they are helping to pay for their children's education, they should have a say in which university their children attend. However, parents' expectations for their children might not always be realistic. Some parents dreamed of their child becoming a doctor, and they told their child what to study.

Natalie said to me that when parents interfere in their children's future, it takes away from them what they want to do; often, millennials will study what their parents want them to because they are scared the parent (or parents) will not pay their tuition, or because they don't want to disappoint their parents. Most students end up changing their major or declare their major once they go to college. It seems that at that point, they feel they have matured and can make a decision on their own; they do not want their parents babying them anymore. As Natalie said, "*You are on your own in college: you pick your own classes, your food, how and where to study, and you realize you are the one doing all this for yourself, and it is your life and future.*"

When I asked Natalie who played the most significant role in their decision as to what to study in college, she responded in the blink of a second by saying, "family." She said there is a difference in the type of parents and their influence on their children. Of her friends, she gave two extreme examples. On one hand, there was Rena's mom, who was the dictator of all Rena's decisions. Then, there was me, Natalie's mom, who said, "*You do what you do as long as it gets you somewhere.*"

Natalie elaborated, "*You will let me decide on what I want to study, and if I decided to change my major, she will make the argument to make sure I am understanding my decision.*"

Natalie bases her knowledge of me on personal experience, when she attended JMU for one year and then decided she wanted to transfer to George Mason. She knew I would not be happy with her change, but she prepared well and presented strongly her case why she wanted to transfer. One of the strong points she highlighted, and sold me on immediately, is that she would save me a good amount of money by moving back home. George Mason is eight minutes by car from our house, and I would not have to pay hundreds of dollars for dorms. Second, George Mason is rated higher in the nursing program than JMU. Three, she was not happy at JMU, but she was not miserable there either. I understood that it is normal for college students in their first year to have trouble adjusting so quickly to being away from home and their friends.

Natalie was seventeen years old when she went to JMU; she needed time to grow and adjust. Ironically, George Mason was my idea in the first place for financial reasons, but Natalie wanted to try the dorm life. Dorms are insanely expensive, and I was against the idea of spending so much for the sake of an experience. However, I liked JMU and knew it was an excellent school. I supported Natalie in making the change, for the reasons she provided and after seeing how hard she worked on the transfer with her advisor at JMU and advisors at George Mason. The only thing I dreaded about the decision was that Natalie would be back living at home, and not taking house chores as seriously as she might if she were on her own.

Nonetheless, Natalie is very helpful with the pets—I give her credit for that. Also, she has a part-time job and is taking care of her daily expenses including some of her college tuition.

## The Role Colleges Play:

Most millennials enter college with a general idea of their major, but sometimes it can take one or two years before a student learns about other majors that could have been a better fit. Unfortunately, those specific majors are not commonly mentioned by counselors or advisors in high school and college.

Natalie knew she wanted to go to nursing school. In her second year, she learned there was a specialty within nursing as a practitioner nurse, which she found interesting, but did not know of previously.

Alissa did not know what she wanted to major in. She took an eight-week course at JMU that introduces students to different majors to help them decide on one. This is a good idea; I encourage all universities to include a similar course, and to urge students to attend even if they already know what major they want to choose. Such a course can broaden a person's perspective, or at the least, confirm that they are on the right track. Tarek learned about interesting majors three years into college, but by then, he felt it was too late to change majors.

Millennials are often scared to change majors. This fear makes them drag in a career that they might not have a passion for instead of stopping and thinking about what they want to do for a living. I know it is costlier for the student and parents to change a major halfway through one studies, but maybe in this situation, a person could add a minor that might take an extra year.

Sometimes it is worth it to pay more in college in order to secure a career that one loves. Another thing one can do after they graduate and begin working is to take courses; some can be certified or others can be traditionally academic such as a master's degree. In my time, experience defined one more so than a degree. I studied English Literature, but taught literature for only two years. I ended up doing more work in management.

Our children need to be prepared for college from elementary school onward. Classes and tests need to be included for children so they can develop an interest in something when they are young. Every time children are asked, "What do you want to be when you grow up?" the response is basic. Often, they want to be like their parents—or, if they love their teacher, they want to become teachers. They look for role models. If children are exposed to more hands-on classes and technical work, they will start developing their personalities, and have a better understanding of what they are good at and where their passions lie. By the time they are in high school, their decision of what to study in college will be easier.

Natalie suggested a solution to help students decide on their major the first year of college. She said colleges should designate hands-on courses to provide undecided students with more information about what majors there are and help them choose. For example, if someone is interested in doing nursing, but not sure, they could shadow a nurse student for a few weeks; next, they could shadow engineering students, and so forth. This would allow students to discover their passions—and be good at it.

Interestingly, a well-known author, of whom I am a fan, thinks along the same lines as Natalie. Napoleon Hill says that everyone needs to take a course in college on making decisions to help them figure out what they want to do; then, they should get tested on that. Students benefit when they major in something out of passion, instead of being influenced by those around them.

# CHAPTER 6

## Millennials and Debt

*In the long run we shall have to pay our debts at a time that may be very inconvenient for our survival."*

~ Norbert Wiener

With the advent of printed material and public schools, each successive generation appears to have more education than their parents. This is certainly true of millennials, the highest educated generation thus far. However, their education is both a blessing and a curse. They sought higher education in the hopes that it would open more doors and provide better job opportunities and higher income. However, according to research, this generation has been particularly affected by the Great Recession. Individuals of this generation move forward with an incredible amount of debt, economic instability, and high unemployment rates.

Due to the necessity of being well educated, millennials end up with large student loans, which tend to hang on because of high unemployment. Then, they struggle to keep up with the lavish lifestyles they have chosen for themselves. The greatest portion of their debt is dedicated to student loans and other basic necessity loans (e.g., car, rent), but the latest studies show that one cause is quickly racing to the top: the "maintenance of social life."

According to a Credit Karma survey from 2018, around 40 percent of millennials are in debt due to spending money they did not have in the first place. They spend heaps of money keeping up with expensive social gatherings, arranging parties, maintaining the nightlife scene, and going on trips.

Sixty-three percent of millennials have more than $10,000 in student debt, according to a survey of 1,000 millennials conducted by Opinion Research Corporation (ORC) International and commissioned by the PR firm PadillaCRT. More than a third of respondents said they owed more than $30,000.

The study shows that for working millennials to be able to pay their debts, they use credit cards to survive each month. They prioritize paying their student and car loans and paying the minimums on their credit cards. According to an article published by Michael Most on HuffPost, "It gets worse. Over half of the millennials who use credit cards not only carry over balances every month, they are charged interest for it and are saddled with additional late fees and the like."

Tuition is rising drastically. Since 1980, prices have tripled at public and private universities and doubled at community colleges. Since then students and their families borrowed more than $106 billion in Federal Direct Loans to attend those institutions. Outstanding student loan debt in the United States in 2017 amounted to over $1.4 trillion, recently surpassing total credit card debt.

Today, millennials cannot live off one income. They need to generate multiple incomes to live a decent life that meets the requirements of their generation. When people who have entered the workforce during a severe economic contraction face prevention of the growth of their earnings, they tend to move their hands in all directions just to earn a living. They shift toward freelancing, odd jobs, and part-time opportunities. Having multiple positions means having less time for personal growth, family bonding, and even taking care of their health.

Parents who have made plans for their children's educations before they were born, or who can financially support their educations, have made life incredibly easier for their children compared to those who have student loans after graduation. Student loan debt is a burden that hunches the backs of new graduates who wants good paying jobs as soon as possible.

Recent graduates with large student loans struggle the hardest. They need jobs that pay enough for them to live modest lives after paying their monthly debts. Their struggle cycles between student loans, credit card payments, rent, commute to and from work, and other bills. They are never satisfied with their income and want to get promoted fast, or else move on to another job.

Some of the people I have interviewed struggle to make ends meet, although not all carry student loans. Millennials in the United States must also worry about paying for health care, unless they are still on their parents' plan. According to the article "5 Ways Millennials View Healthcare Differently," from the University of Chicago, millennials understand that the U.S. healthcare system doesn't work for everybody. Unlike their parents and grandparents, many think that health care is a right as opposed to a privilege.

Health care in the States can be expensive. A 2015 study showed that 50 percent of all millennials did not have a family doctor. Fortunately, however, data from a 2016 Health Survey showed that all but 11 percent of millennials had health insurance. Although they did not tend to have a lot of health problems, the problems that did pop up were related to weight, depression, or anxiety.

Chances are, if someone works at a nonprofit organization or has not earned distinction in a profession or major like IT, engineering, law, or medicine, their salary may not exceed $35,000 to $45,000. This income is not sufficient to live a decent basic life. Millennials are either just surviving or carrying more debt on credit cards to be able to enjoy a vacation or a better quality of life. In big cities, millennials still live like they did during their college years, by renting a space with a bunch of other people to manage costs.

Millennials need to learn how to make decisions to change their outcomes. As difficult as a situation might seem, it is better to figure out a solution while still young than to carry a greater financial burden at a later age. Maybe buying a house is not a priority over paying off loans. Millennials: it is worth your time to reflect on yourselves. Try to ask yourself if you like your job. Do you wake up in the morning excited to go to work? Is this what you want to do for years to come? Figure out what your passion is and start taking courses and educate yourself in that field. This could be a way to change your life and income.

Mike put it simply: "*We are a socially active generation and stand up for social injustice. We are not happy with wages and barely making enough to meet the expensive life and debts we carry. We are a well-educated generation but cannot afford to buy a house. Improve wages for millennials to be able to build a life and family.*"

Many millennials I worked with and interviewed told me they have a side job in addition to their full-time job because their salary is not enough. Tarek drives for Uber as a side job to help pay off his student loans. Even though Tarek is an engineer and makes a relatively good income, his net profit after taxes and other deductions is only enough to pay rent, loans, gas, and other key expenses. Mike does translation on the side because his income from a nonprofit organization is barely enough to live off. Sandy works on weekends in a retail store to make ends meet.

I do not blame millennials if they live with their parents for many years after graduating from college. They are blessed to have caring parents who are willing to take them in and care for them in times of difficulty and tough economic conditions. Millennials do not live with their parents because they are spoiled or dependent. Society has not left them other options. Education is costly; millennials are focused on it as a means to a better career and a better financial life. Ironically, education has brought them debt, financial dependency on their parents, and jobs with long hours. Hopefully, down the road, millennials will catch up, pay off their debts, and be able to make a decent living at jobs they enjoy—or at a series of jobs they find gratifying.

# CHAPTER 7
## Time for Work

*"We can each define ambition and progress for ourselves.*
*The goal is to work toward a world where expectations are*
*not set by the stereotypes that hold us back, but by our*
*personal passion, talents and interests."*

~ Sheryl Sandberg

Finding jobs, managing work with very little solid job experience, and dealing with situations in my professional life are all reasons that made me want to write this book. Not only did I go through this with my children, but also as a manager for many years, I saw millennials struggling at their jobs on many levels, with minimal guidance from their supervisors.

## Finding Jobs

Millennials cannot wait until they graduate from college. They believe that the life ahead of them is the life they dream of. They are raised to think that a degree will guarantee a good job. A good job will provide good income, and a good salary will enable them to live a good financial life. It sounds about right, although there are other ways to make money and be successful. What millennials are not told is that finding a job with limited experience is not easy and might take some time. Then, after securing a job, there is the entire process through which one has to grow and become experienced in a career. Our companies are designed so that employees have to jump up the ladder, step by step. By the time millennials reach the top, they will have devoted years of hard work and living on a tight budget.

University's role in preparing students for the workforce is limited. There are many things a student needs to know before he or she graduates and secures a job. Millennials rely on online sources and try to maneuver around the job-hunting process until they succeed. My family and I learned this the hard way. Tarek said, *"Colleges have a list of hundreds of companies with one paragraph about each, but you are at an age where you don't know what kind of a job you want, and you end up applying for all jobs close to your major."* At an age when they have very little professional experience, millennials tend to look at jobs primarily from the salary perspective and then, maybe, look into the reputation of the workplace—regardless if it is the best fit or the ideal job. Tarek adds, *"Millennials are not taught to think and make decisions, and then we find ourselves needing to make a major decision about our future by finding a job and being on our own."*

Most millennials work hard during their college years by having side jobs and internships. After spending sixteen or more years of one's life earning an education, one would assume that would provide all the tools necessary to join the workforce—but then they are slammed with reality. I remember when my children could not wait to graduate and start working. They thought once they began working, they would earn money and be free to live the lives they wanted.

Of course, I let them believe that because deep down, I thought that their era was better than mine. I did not want to project any of my negativity from past experiences on them. It never dawned on me that finding a job in today's world would be more challenging for a millennial than for someone my age. I believed that baby boomers struggled to find jobs because they were competing with a younger generation. I also thought because there are so many websites to apply through, along with countless other sources, millennials had it easy. However, it seems the more options one has, the more competition there is.

With today's technology, it is easy to *apply* for jobs. That does not mean it is easy to get a job. There are many websites designed for career searching where one can narrow down the position of interest that matches their area of specialty. For example, if one wants a job as a program assistant, they can enter that in the search box, choose the city or geographic area of interest, and hit search. They will get many options for jobs that they can look through and apply to. After that, they can just type in their information and credentials.

Another way to search for jobs is through job fairs that take place frequently at colleges. Typically, these job fairs are announced ahead of time, and colleges will post about it. Recruiters from different companies come to college campuses, and students have a chance to speak to them and give out their resume, or apply on the company's website once they have a better understanding of what the company does.

Of the many millennials I spoke with, most use LinkedIn and school websites, in addition to job fairs on campus. LinkedIn is more helpful for those with a few years of experience, but it still is an option for new graduates. The more experience a person has, the more likely recruiters and HR personnel are to reach out to them about applying for jobs at their companies. I advise readers to have a LinkedIn profile and keep it up-to-date.

Finding a job can be a full-time job on its own—and a strenuous one. Searching for jobs, applying, making sure that one understands and meets all requirements , writing a professional cover letter that will stand out, and attaching a well-written resume is a lot of work. I know many college graduates who applied for over a hundred positions before getting an interview or an offer.

Internships are a great way to start a career. I encourage students to take at least one internship their junior or senior year of college. The subject one studies is very important, but applying this knowledge is even more critical. Working with millennials, I noticed those who did internships found jobs more easily—sometimes at the same place they interned. Those who didn't obtain internships struggled to land jobs quickly.

An internship prepares a person well for the workforce. Those who join the workforce directly after college without an internship might struggle more to get the hang of the work. It is natural for a person to take time adapting to new tasks and a new environment, especially when the environment is so competitive. I have noticed in the different places I have worked that employers expect employees to be quick learning their ways. If an employee does not demonstrate those skills from the beginning, managers tend to judge them, which impedes the employee's professional development and growth.

Mike shared his experience on preparing for job interviews. He said, "*I made a bad decision by applying for jobs after I graduated because I wanted to focus on my studying. I got an offer after three months of graduating. I applied online through Indeed. I didn't network, and I didn't know a lot of people so 'getting it online' was my only option. University websites were not very effective. I wrote my own resume by taking the time to think of my weaknesses and strengths. Then I looked for jobs that matched my strengths. I applied for more than 200 jobs until I got one job offer. The economy was bad in 2012. In the job interview, most questions were about my work experience, and I didn't have much at that time. I prepared well before the interview by searching online the type of questions for interviews and reviewed people's responses to the questions. I prepared so well for interviews and presented my responses with strength."*

I worked with Mike. He is very good at his job. But millennials are sometimes caught in the impossible position of having to navigate an interview by providing experiential knowledge that they have not acquired yet to get a job.

It sounds like Mike did not take long to get a job. However, he applied for a large number of jobs and got only one offer, which is typical for someone who does not have previous work or internship experience.

I can shed light on some difficulties my son faced when he was looking for a job. Tarek's experience might be helpful to understand that they are not alone, and nothing is wrong with them. Tarek's experience might also be useful to those who are about to graduate by allowing them to skip some of those challenges.

According to a post on the Virginia Tech website, "Sixty percent of Virginia Tech's 2013-14 graduates who responded to a university survey are employed or have a job offer, while 23 percent are continuing their education, according to a recently released report."

Tarek spent nine months without succeeding at getting even a single job offer. He started applying for jobs through job fairs while he was still at VT, in addition to the school website and job websites. Then he graduated and kept applying for jobs, thinking that he would land at least an interview. Eventually, he got a few interviews, but he never heard back. After two months, he started getting concerned. He contacted his friends and classmates. Some of them had gotten jobs they did not like, while others had not gotten jobs at all, just like him. That made him feel better to know that he was not alone, and that eventually, he would get a job.

Meanwhile, Tarek decided to work as a waiter to generate some income while he was job hunting. Weeks turned into months, and soon it had been five months since he had heard from any of the jobs he had applied for.

One day he said to me sadly, "*Was it worth going to college if I was going to end up being a waiter?*" I was heartbroken to hear him giving up. Of course, my motherly instincts told me to start helping him find jobs. I would spend hours in front of the computer looking for jobs for industrial engineers, but all I would see were jobs that required three to five years of experience. Even when I searched for intermediate positions, I still got jobs requiring one or more years of experience. I thought, What the heck is this? How do they expect someone to find a job when they just graduated with only a few days' experience? Even I started believing that my son would never get a job, and he would spend the rest of his life waiting tables when he wanted so much to work in his field; but, as I mentioned earlier, after nine months, Tarek got a desirable job close to VT.

That is how a lot of millennials accept jobs: they accept the offer, which, in most cases, is the only offer, so they have nothing to compare it with. They take jobs out of desperation, not, "Is this the type of work I would like to be doing?" Or "Is this the kind of work that will help me learn and grow? Is this the job that I can last in for at least a few years?"

Just to be clear, Tarek wasn't applying for a new job because he was miserable at his former job—quite the contrary. The job was not bad, but he hated living in the suburbs so far away from the city life and his girlfriend, who was living in Richmond. She was working at Amazon, and her job was too good to quit and move to the South, where Tarek was. Tarek spent most of his weekends driving four hours one way to visit his girlfriend or to visit us in Northern Virginia. For a year and a half, Tarek applied for job after job until he got bored and frustrated. If applying for jobs was a specialty, Tarek would be the master. I knew he was good at his job. The testament to that was not only his promotion, but his leadership of a quality control department in his company that was challenging to manage. Tarek's manager's evaluation at the end of the year was incredible. Why, then, was Tarek still not getting job offers? Here are some reasons we finally figured out as a family why Tarek might have had difficulty finding a job:

**1. Job Search:**

As I mentioned previously, the online platforms for job announcements are countless. Applying can be overwhelming. With time, candidates feel the websites that work for them best. Of course, I am not trying to insinuate that candidates will spend a long time applying for jobs, but they will find some website that is more relevant to their experience than ones that require years of experience. For example, Mike mentioned that Indeed.com worked well for him. I applied often on their website, but never was called in for an interview. On the other hand, I was very lucky with LinkedIn and got several job interviews, while several of my colleagues told me it had never worked for them. University websites worked for a few students who got responses at least for interviews, and some got jobs. Broadening one's options by applying as often as possible gives one a better chance.

Connecting and networking with people you know can be a plus. Connections work wonders in the U.S. If a person knows someone working at a place they are interested in and they care about the person, they can pave the person's way inside—or, at least, for an interview. Small non-profits prefer to hire staff and board member referrals, rather than outsiders.

I know sometimes pride or fear of rejection stands in the way. I saw this happen with my children when they were looking for jobs. They preferred to struggle on their own than ask for help. Yet, a few of my coworkers got jobs through connections and so did I. I was called in for an interview. Once that door was open, the rest was on me. I prepared well for the interview and presented myself with strength. Several months after I got the job, I learned that another person almost got the offer, but when the company interviewed me, they were more impressed by my skills than the other candidates.

It is important not to give up on applying for jobs. It is so frustrating, but one also needs to be patient. They must believe in themselves and their skills. When one looks for jobs with the attitude that they will get not only a job, but their dream job, I believe it will happen. One attracts what one thinks of. If one thinks positively, one will get positive results.

Once Tarek started believing and practicing positivity, he got three job interviews and two offers. It was a wonderful dilemma for us as a family when we had to discuss which job he should accept when previously Tarek had not received any job offers. This was a new situation for us. We needed a service that could help us choose the best job. But such a service did not exist, so we had to rely on our common sense and instincts for recognizing pros and cons of each job, and, ultimately, let Tarek decide what he wanted. All it took was for Tarek to take a three-day seminar on self-development and positive thinking. One might think it is a hoax, but try it. What is there to lose? If someone is spending time worrying and living in fear of not getting a job, they might as well do the opposite.

## 2. Resume:

Trying to figure out the secret to a good resume? It's really just making your resume subjective: based on who is reading it, as Sandy put it. Tarek's resume was not as good as he thought it was. I guess it was not enough to search online for resume templates and mimic them. For sure, no one is born with good resume writing skills, and it is something that isn't taught. I struggled with my resume many times before I realized resumes are not something that people write often enough to become good at. I suggested to Tarek that he send his resume to an expert for improvement. Tarek paid $150 for the service and got an impressive resume in return. Not only was the resume written and formatted better, but it included keywords from the electronic screening system that most companies use. Who would have known that companies do not have time to manually screen the massive number of resumes they receive for every job posting—or that companies use an electronic system to search for keywords? And even if we had known, how would we have been able to figure out what the keywords were? The online services that write resumes use the same system in testing customers' resumes for keywords to make sure their resumes will pop up when they apply for a job. It sure worked for Tarek. That is how he landed his second job.

## 3. Cover Letter:

It is crucial to write a cover letter that addresses the qualifications in the job announcement. In other words, a cover letter should sell a candidate's skills and show what makes him or her stand out from the crowd of competitors. A candidate needs to show the company why they should hire them, and only them. The cover letter must be professional and perfectly written. Spelling mistakes or grammatical errors give the recruiter the impression that a candidate is not detailed, not professional, and, worst of all, not serious about the job. This was a weakness in Tarek's cover letters. He had never written one before, and he needed direction to start. He went to Google and searched for "cover letter samples" and "templates." Those were useful tools, but not enough. Templates are generic; cover letters need more work in order to look professional, sincere, and catchy.

The other challenge is using professional terms in one's own language. Sometimes, the job description itself can be helpful to take terms and ideas the company uses. After Tarek realized his cover letters were not tailored well enough to each job, he sent his draft to a professional to write a standard cover letter. The language, the terms, and a clear sense of who he is, professionally and academically, were there; he just needed to work around them to fit the job description he was applying for. The application process was easier once he completed the resume and cover letter, both of which are time-consuming and can hurt a job opportunity if not done well.

### 4. Submitting Your Application:

Imagine that a candidate now has a good resume and an attractive looking cover letter. Now, he or she needs to send the application to the job of interest. The first important point is to look at the deadline for submission. Recruiters always post in the job announcement the closing date for accepting applications. Most likely, they will not consider an application if it is even a single hour late. Secondly, it is key to attach or upload resumes and cover letters in the format instructed by the job post. For example, some jobs ask candidates to attach documents as .pdf files. Also, some companies provide instructions on what to write in the subject line of the email if attaching documents. Candidates must make sure to read instructions carefully. I once applied for a job that asked me to add a code for the post and expected me to put it in the subject line of the email, along with the title of the position they provided. If one does not read instructions carefully and fails to do what the company wants, the company will disregard your application. This shows how much effort candidates need to put into reading the instructions, and how they need to take their time so as to be efficient. I know when candidates are applying for many jobs, they get tired and start applying quickly because they just want to get it over with. Don't sit behind the computer submitting dozens of applications back to back. Take a break in between each application, even if it is for five minutes. Eat, grab a snack, or walk the dog.

### 5. Network:

I believe college is not only a place for education, but an excellent place for networking. Students are there for four or five years. During that time, they meet people from different regions within the United States and the world. Students should make good connections with their peers and professors, who can be useful in the future. Many peers, especially those who have similar majors, will end up getting jobs and can be a source of reference.

Tarek invested more in making friends with international students, who ended up going back to their countries after graduation. He lacked local connections. He learned this a bit late, but he made up for it at his job by networking with his colleagues and building good relations. It also helps not to burn bridges with others in college in case of running into them at a job one day. One never knows. That person could be the one to interview you for that job.

I remember once a girl was hired at my organization for an interim position. A few weeks later, we hired another girl for another interim position. The two girls turned out to know each other very well from college and had stepped on each other's toes in such a way that they both held grudges. One of them lacked professional workplace judgment. She didn't realize that she shouldn't tell anyone else about her dispute with the other girl (which is how I knew about their issue). Luckily, she only told me, and I gave her my two cents. I explained to her that we did not care to take sides, but we would judge her attitude.

I would give others the same advice: be professional with your colleagues, and if you decide to leave your job, leave it on good terms. What goes around comes around. We live in a small world, and we will run into people we worked with in another job, or someone they know. Always be professional and a good person. It will take you far.

In Dale Carnegie's posthumous book, *How to Win Friends and Influence People in the Digital Age*, Carnegie recommends that everyone abide by the following rules: 1. Do not criticize, condemn, or complain about another person; 2. Show respect for colleagues; and 3. Always try to put oneself in the other person's shoes. Do not gossip about other people. Be a collaborator at the office.

### 6. Dress code:

Candidates need to dress professionally for an interview. It gives an impression of how serious they are about the interview and about the job. If one looks good, one will feel good. It is always better for men to wear a suit and women to wear a blazer or suit jacket. It is important that the suit fits well and is comfortable; it should be clean, neat, and pressed. Men should avoid wearing flashy ties and loud colors.

I go for comfort over flashiness. Honestly, if one's clothes or shoes are uncomfortable, it controls the mind during the interview.

Some companies tell candidates the dress code for the interview. I was once part of a team interviewing candidates for an interim position. Three of the final candidates came dressed nicely, but not professionally. I don't mean they were dressed badly, but they did not have a suit or jacket on. When the interviews were over, the first thing HR commented on was how they dressed. I was surprised. I was impressed with one of the candidates and did not want the group to make this decision based on dress code, but rather because of the applicant's accurate responses and her personality. I fought hard for her, and she got the job. I noticed from those interviews that millennials are not necessarily aware of the dress code for interviews. Some think if they are dressed nicely, that is what counts. Unfortunately, that is not the way it always is. Candidates must do the research on how to dress for an interview. They can find helpful tips on Google, and they can always ask people who have already gone through the process.

Some younger people have tattoos or nose or lip rings. If a candidate is applying for a job with a large, conservative company, they should cover tattoos until they get a good feel for the work environment. Ditto for nose rings: candidates might want to take them out. This may not be necessary if the candidate is applying for a job with a music recording studio or if they are an artist. They should use good judgment about the company and the interview and take it seriously.

### 7. Interview:

Congratulations! The candidate has been noticed. Their resume and cover letter has attracted the recruiter. Now, the candidate must prepare for the opportunity. Confidence comes with growth and experience. It is hard to be relaxed and confident in an interview. Psychologically, the feeling of being questioned is scary, especially if one is desperate for the job. The key is to relax before going into an interview. This is by far the most straight-forward advice anyone can give you, but it's also the best. I used to tell my children, "Sleep well, eat a good breakfast, and take deep breaths in and out as often as you can." I also recommend chamomile. For some reason, it helps me relax. I have found that talking to myself—saying affirmations out loud or in my head—helps. A candidate should tell themselves how amazing they are, how experienced they are, how relaxed they are, how they will do a great job at the interview, and the interviewers will be so impressed that they will call the next day to offer them the job. Even if it doesn't work out, it is always nice to praise oneself for the effort. I like a saying by James Allen, which goes like this: "As a man thinketh in his heart so is he."

When a person is a recent graduate, and has no previous work experience to build off, it is difficult to elaborate on answers in an interview. Usually, when one has experience, they can think of the questions being asked, relate them to a past situation, and support their answers with examples. When a person does not have previous experience, or their experience is typical of that of a young person, they must rely more on what they learned in college, common sense and, most importantly, their instinct. Sitting in front of people that are waiting to judge is tough; no one likes to be judged based on their looks or what they say. However, this is the way to get a job. Going into the interview prepared is what helps control nerves and provide more confidence.

Unfortunately, companies and organizations do not take youth and inexperience into consideration when they prepare generic questions for their interviews. This weakness needs to be addressed and taken seriously by firms. Recruiters and HR personnel should look into interview questions and make sure that when they are interviewing for an interim position, they are focusing on personality and analytical thinking, rather than on experience.

Lots of online resources can prepare a candidate for interviews. Sometimes, if the interview is with a big corporation, one can find interview questions that are specific to that firm online. One also can discover many online references on how to prepare for interviews in specific fields.

In college, students should take advantage of the opportunity if their school offers mock interviews. Another option is to do mockup interviews with other professionals. Many lovely professionals will agree to meet, talk over the phone, or share tips for the interview. One of the things that Tarek mastered was reading in depth about what the company to which he was applying did, and his role in the firm. He would prepare good questions to ask in the interview, showcasing how much he knew about their work. This frequently impresses interviewers and makes a candidate look well prepared.

I know how it feels when a person gets the email thanking them for their interest, but regretfully relating that they have not been selected for the position and wishing them good luck. That really sucks—especially if the person felt as though they did well in the interview, and the company provided no reasons for why they were not selected. They are left to wonder on their own, "What could I have done better?" Sometimes, the reasons can be as seemingly inconsequential as the way they dressed for the interview. If they were dressed nicely, but not professionally, this could be an issue. Other times, the person might not be selected, not because they weren't good, but because someone else was better. That other person might have had the same lack of experience, but she or he was better prepared for the interview and presented themselves with more confidence.

Sandy believes that Human Resource practices are outdated. When she reads job descriptions and believes they apply perfectly to her experience and skills, yet she is not called for an interview—or the "interview" consists of three basic questions that do not allow an accurate assessment of her skills—she becomes disappointed.

Candidates: just don't give up. Keep learning from every interview.

**8. References:**

This is the most challenging part of the job process. I suffered from it. My children suffered from it, and a number of people have told me how they almost lost their job opportunities because they could not find three references. It is easy to get one reference—perhaps a professor or an internship supervisor—but getting three references (they cannot be family members) is hard. It is tough, but companies insist on it. Which is why I say: do not burn bridges. Some people give the names of fictitious managers—friends or family members who own businesses and can claim one worked for them— as references, but that is risky and I do not encourage it.

I have acted as a reference for a number of my colleagues. When I got the call, the questions were precise. It is difficult to fabricate answers if one is providing a reference for someone who has not worked for him or her. It helps to volunteer or do internships in college. Later on, one can use those connections as references.

**9. Location:**

Sometimes, a person might be looking for a job in the wrong geographical area. They should ask themselves: am I willing to relocate where there are more job opportunities for my area of specialty? Washington D.C. and Virginia, where my family and I live, is not a great area for engineers unless they want to be contractors for consulting firms and the government or be located in a remote area. This was one of the obstacles that Tarek faced. He had more job opportunities in the Midwest, but he did not want to relocate, so he had to be more patient in finding a job in our area.

Sandy moved from the New York area to D.C. for college. After college, she did not face issues finding a job because she did an internship and got a job offer with the same organization. However, she faced challenges finding a job after three years of experience. She was very good at what she did and had been promoted twice. She lasted three years at her job before she realized she was no longer motivated, and needed to seek a different opportunity where she could grow and develop. It took Sandy two years of applying for jobs without any hope for an offer. Finally, for family reasons, she was forced to relocate to another state, and there she was able to find a job quickly. When I told her, "*You are lucky it worked for you,*" she said, "*I think it is a small state and they do not have many people with my experience. I had less competition in that state than in Washington D.C.*"

She could be right; Sandy was competing with many professionals with master's degrees in International Affairs within the District of Columbia. She told me, "*In the D.C. area, having a master's degree is like having a bachelor's degree; everyone has it. A master's Degree is not unique anymore like it used to be decades ago.*" She added, "*Monkeys can do the job we are doing, but for some reason master's is a requirement. I do not understand why. But it seems that organizations in this area know that it is competitive and try to raise the bar high.*"

I met a woman from Jordan who had flown all the way to Washington D.C. to network for job opportunities. I thought, "Poor Suzie. She will never get a job that way." What intrigued me about Suzie the most was her confidence. She had no work permit in the U.S. Her experience for twenty or so years was in management. She was not familiar with the work culture in the United States. I asked her how she planned to get a job if she was not a citizen. She told me, "*I'm looking for an organization to sponsor my work permit.*" All the odds were against her, yet she was telling me what she planned to do as if it were normal.

A few days later, Suzie emailed me to see if I wanted to meet for lunch or coffee. We went out for coffee, and she looked tired. I asked her if everything was okay. To my surprise she said, "*I have been meeting with senior management from different organizations back to back. I am tired, but I networked so well.*" The people and organizations she met with were ones I had applied to in the past, but never heard back from. Suzi was able to meet them in person and market her skills. At the end of the discussion, she said, *"Before I decided to come to D.C., I applied for 400 jobs in the United States and did not hear from one."*

"Wow," was all I could say. Long before technology, this is how people used to apply for jobs: by walking into the place and asking to talk to a manager. Could it still be effective? It worked for Suzie.

# CHAPTER 8

## Challenges Millennials Face at Work

*"Choose a job you love, and
you will never have to work a day in your life"*

~ Confucius

Millennials want a career, not just a job. They have high expectations, but less patience. They want to advance in their careers quickly, whereas previous generations understood that advancement in a job may occur slowly.

Cathy is from Generation X. She stuck with her first job at a large nonprofit for more than twenty years. She started as an intern, then got a job there, doing the same work for decades—until, one day, she realized she needed to move on. She landed a government job that she thought was a better fit. Cathy told me, *"I wish I knew what millennials know today; keep changing jobs and going up until you find your place."* She added, *"My generation grew up believing that the longer you stick in a job, the more loyal you are to the place of work."* Cathy admires millennials and how they stand up for their rights when they see something in the workforce that they do not like. If they cannot change it, they will move on to another job.

Until now, baby boomers and Generation X have held high positions and managed millennials. The majority of them have been in the same workplace for more than ten years. The older generations seem less understanding and less tolerant of millennials in the workforce. Instead of developing with time, they blame the younger generations for not understanding how to do things "right," i.e., the old way. Millennials are still figuring out the management style that suits them best. They face difficulties understanding and accepting the past generation's style. Different generations are working together, but the gap remains enormous.

Mike, a millennial, believes that although millennials are new to the workforce, smart, and highly educated, they lack professional skills. He said, "*I see my generation struggle juggling between a number of tasks and becoming stressed out. They end up working long hours to catch up with work and figure out things on their own. Of course, if managers spend some time to guide them, I'm sure they will learn faster and be more productive. They might even last longer at their job.*"

Mike told me: "*When I started my job, I was not trained at all. I was thrown immediately in work. My manager was traveling, and I just sat until I was given tasks. The first day at 9 a.m., I was asked to work on a workshop with no guidance. Next day, I was asked to write proposals without giving me any information or idea on what its content was about. Even my coworkers, who are from my generation, were not interested in supporting or guiding me. I considered resigning so many times, but I didn't like the idea of giving up.*"

By asking millennials how they knew what to do when they first started their jobs, I received different answers. Sandy thinks personality plays a role. She said, "*If you are a motivated person "Type A," already organized, and driven to do things correctly, that helps a lot. But training is definitely important.*" For example, understanding how to address and correspond with different audiences is something a person might not know on his or her own. They need guidance.

Maggie, on the other hand, did not struggle in most of her jobs. She had worked in restaurants since she was fifteen years old, and she gained lots of experience over the years managing other employees. In college, she interned in a number of places related to her area of study.

Maggie gained so much experience that when she started her first official job after graduation, she did it well. She relied on her skills, but also asked and learned from others. She was promoted in the same organization three times. Maggie was in the right field of work, entirely related to her degree. People like Maggie, however, are rare. The majority of millennials struggle if they do not have guidance.

# Manager`s Role

Managers have challenging jobs. They have to meet their goals, continuously prove their abilities, and ensure their team is meeting deadlines with full efficiency. Any mistake a team member makes is on the manager. This is why managers are stressed out most of the time. Sometimes, that stress reflects negatively on their team. A competent, strong manager is one who is always composed and signals that everything is under control, even when it is not. These are the managers who look for solutions, rather than react and blame. They are the ones who identify their staff's weaknesses and work with them to improve. That is the ideal manager to work for. They are out there in almost every workplace, but sometimes we do not notice them as much as we notice the weak managers, who lose control from the first hiccup.

I don't believe the amount of experience one has makes a successful manager. I have worked in a place where two managers were baby boomers, close in age. One was calm and in control, whereas the other one would freak out over everything. Ironically, the one who freaked out had managed more people in her career, yet she failed to lead a team without driving them away. Attitude and personality are two main factors of being a successful manager. Sometimes, a subject matter expert is taken away from their subject and put into a management position. The person might lose confidence, and struggle to keep up the excellent work that she or he had been able to do before. The idea of failing and getting fired might become their nightmare, and they might start reacting with volatile moods, confusing their staff.

Managers keep an employee happy or miserable. They are like teachers in school. A good teacher explains his or her subject well, makes students like the subject, and makes the subject easy to understand. Most likely, students will do well in his or her class because they enjoy learning. In college, students rate professors based on how well the professor has explained the topic. When students want to sign up for a course, they can look at the professor's rating to help them decide if they should sign up with that professor or go with another.

I have encountered amazing managers who are experts in their field and good mentors at the same time. These managers are the best to work for, especially for a young employee who wants someone to mentor and coach them in their starting career.

I have mentored a number of millennials in my career, and I felt their struggle, insecurity, and lack of confidence. They fear making mistakes, and they fear making a decision. At the same time, they fear asking for help, for they are afraid that doing so will show weakness or incompetence. This all goes back to the type of manager a millennial gets. Some managers like employees who ask questions; others want their employees to complete tasks in a more self-directed fashion. I know many millennials who spend a great deal of time trying to figure out a task, rather than asking for guidance.

Once an employee learns how to do a task, it becomes easier for them to do it again. They will no longer need to go back and ask (*that* is when they might be seen as incompetent.) One of the tips I have shared is to write down the steps of a task as if creating guidelines for others who are new, just as they were once. I have noticed that some millennials do not bother to write down things the first time or for follow up. Relying on memory is impressive, but once there are too many tasks, relying on memory can become difficult—especially when one must prioritize tasks.

At one of my jobs, we worked with Iraqi scientists; most of the scientists in Iraq hold a doctor title and like to be addressed as "Dr. So and So". Most North American medical doctors prefer to be addressed as "Dr." as well, but this is particularly important in the Iraqi culture. One of the millennials, John—newly hired for an interim position—was asked to draft an email to "Dr. Ali" following up on his travel arrangements. John had never worked in the region and did not understand the culture and protocols within Iraq's scientific community. He began his email by plainly saying, "Dear Ali, would you kindly send me your resume?"

I was copied on the email along with his manager. When I read the email, I felt a crunch in my stomach. I imagined Dr. Ali reading the email and feeling insulted or offended.

One must understand their audience and respect their culture. John never intended to be disrespectful; in fact, he believed he did a great job sending the email. It was just a lack of guidance from his manager. I waited for some time, hoping John's manager, who was sitting next to me and had just read John's email, would pay attention, but there was no reaction. I got up and said to him in a soft tone, not intending to embarrass him, "*John, just to let you know, Iraqi scientists hold the title of doctor and like to be addressed with it. Also, when you start an email with Iraqis, say something like 'I hope you are doing well.' They find our emails dry culturally.*" That was it. John did what I told him and realized later that these tips were essential in dealing with people of different cultures.

Young employees with minimal experience do not know these cultural things, but a manager who has been working in this field should pay attention to her team. However, it seems some managers don't know how to give feedback. They just want to make sure things are done and check them off their list. Some managers are weak and are afraid of being seen as bossy or mean—which, ironically is how they end up being seen anyway. There is something called constructive criticism where one can give another feedback in a good, positive way without offending. I read a funny quote once that said, "Diplomacy is the ability to tell someone to 'go to hell' in such a way that he looks forward to the trip."

## Don't Work for the Bully

Unfortunately, there is always that one person at work who will make someone hate their job. I have bumped into a few in my life where I wished many times I could open the window and throw them out. Thank God that in the U.S., windows in buildings do not open. I guess there is some precedent of people thinking like me. It is so unfair that one person can make the work environment so toxic. I have never understood why senior management often takes no action to get rid of or reprimand toxic people.

One probably wonders why the toxic person behaves the way they do in the first place. Well, I can be a psychologist for a minute and give many reasons, but one is enough: a toxic manager is incompetent and lacks confidence in themselves and their skills. They are no different from bullies. No one should agree to work for a bully. Unfortunately, many of us end up working for them—and leaving the job because of them. High turnover on its own is a signal to senior management that something is wrong.

The solutions to having a healthy work environment and keeping staff happy are straightforward if taken seriously by senior management. Millennials tend to see most of their managers as bad. This could be due to intimidation, or it could be that millennials want to be perfect, and have difficulty taking feedback as a vehicle for improvement. It could also be a lack of work satisfaction. They tend to blame that on managers too. No matter what the reasons, management needs to have an open-door policy where they encourage staff to express their opinions—and millennials need to stand and speak up.

It is important for all employees, including millennials, to express their thoughts in a constructive manner. This increases the chance of being happy on the job. Gossiping and accusing are not a solution and only add to the toxicity of the workplace. There is a solution to every problem if one looks for answers and avoids blaming and driving themselves to the point where they hate their job. Wherever one goes for work, there will always be something or someone to make him or her unhappy. They cannot keep running away from conflict. If one does, he or she will run from personal issues as well. To grow and mature professionally or on a personal level, one needs to learn how to see the solution to a problem. Expressing opinions in the right way can be a start.

Dena was working at a very small nonprofit organization where it was only her, her boss, and an intern who came in a couple of days a week. Dena had already gone through tough times in her life after she lost her husband, as I described previously. It took Dena more than two years to heal and be able to function again. We thought a small office environment would be a good fit for her mental state.

Dena was not ready to deal with stress, and I did not want her to either, but having a routine can be healing. I never thought any person on earth could be so heartless to a young woman who had gone through so much, was doing her work to the best of her abilities, and was so sweet in her soul—but I was wrong. To say that her boss was difficult would have been a gross understatement. This boss had a temper and became angry and impatient with her employees. She had no respect for people around her and would insult and hurt Dena each day. Dena lived in fear and stress for nine months. She often would share with me what was going on, and I would advise her on what to do, but nothing worked. Then, Dena started responding to her boss when she mistreated her, or ignoring her boss when she had her tantrums.

One day, I met Dena by the metro to go home together, because we worked in the same area. As she was walking toward me, I saw a broken girl walking as if the weight of the world was on her shoulders. I thought to myself, "*I wonder what went wrong today.*" When Dena got close to me, I asked her, "*What is wrong?*" She responded breathlessly, as if she could not inhale: "*I can't do this anymore. I think I might have a heart attack.*" Her boss had thrown a document at her—which almost sliced her face—and told her, "*I want you to finish this work today.*" My heart pounded with anger and sadness. How could anyone be so mean—and why?

If Dena was not doing her job well, fire her; but why keep her and abuse her? I told Dena, *"Tomorrow, you go to work and quit. But tonight, you prepare your resignation and say exactly why you are quitting. Professionally list all the things this boss did to you and send it to her and the chairman of the board."*

Dena did precisely that. When she went to work the next day, she was freaking out. She was so scared of facing her boss and telling her she was quitting. When her boss walked into the office that day, Dena sat behind her desk with her coat on and her purse in her lap. Her boss immediately started rudely giving orders. Dena looked at her and said, *"I'm not going to do the work you asked me to do because I quit. You are rude, mean, and awful to work for."* Dena walked out of the building shaking. She hit send on the resignation email she had prepared the night before. Then she called me and told me in a shaky voice that she had quit. I told her, *"Congratulations. I'm so proud of you."*

Dena's email to the chairman turned out to be great. The chairman called Dena and spoke to her for a whole hour to gather detailed information on what happened. He thanked Dena for her honesty and promised her he would follow up on this issue with full seriousness. Dena felt triumphant, and today she has her own online business and is so happy.

Dena could have quit and not informed the chairman about the conflict she had with the boss. The company would have hired another person and the manager would have mistreated him or her. It turned out, six people before Dena had quit in less than two years for the same reasons, but never bothered to tell the board. The chairman felt there was something wrong in the office but could not put a finger on the issue because no one was talking. Dena's email not only helped the board to understand what was going on, but she also saved others from enduring a similar situation.

I want to share Dena's experience in the hopes that people will realize they can do a lot for themselves and others if they understand their options. No one has the right to "use and abuse" a system. We should not allow such people to get away with evil behavior.

So many people are afraid to stand up because they think they will get fired or never get a recommendation for another job. This is nonsense! One should never let thoughts like these stand in the way of one's happiness professionally. Even if the person gets fired, there are better options than being in an abusive environment. If there is no HR department at a workplace, one can do what Dena did—tell the CEO, Chairman, another manager, or seek legal advice.

That being said, I am not promoting the "tell action." I am only talking about bullying and abuse in the workplace, which is entirely unacceptable. If options exist to complain to someone, that should be the first way to go. In Dena's situation, there was no one to talk to. She had only learned about the option of telling the chairman a few days before she quit, when she went to an event with him and got to know him. She told me that he was such a nice person, unlike what her boss had said about him. I suggested that she reach out to him when she decided to quit, so that he would know and hopefully do something about it for the sake of the organization.

In a bigger workplace, there are other people to talk to, but in reality, abuse occurs less often in larger places than smaller ones. People at bigger places know that they cannot get away with things as easily as they might in a small place. That doesn't mean abuse and bullying do not exist in larger workplaces, but options to deal with it are more numerous.

This leads me to the discussion of HR. Most workplaces have HR departments on-site or as contractors; employees should have their contacts in case they need to talk. However, HR people are not always qualified to deal with issues in the right way, especially if the staff member goes about it the wrong way to begin with. HR tends to protect managers more than staff unless there are serious allegations, such as sexual harassment. One should always go to HR prepared and professional.

A good management structure can improve working conditions. Here are some suggestions from personal experience and recommendations from millennials:

## Internal Communication

Internal communication is one of the major problems in the workforce. Often, managers do not communicate important updates well to their staff, and they fail to give clear instructions on assigned tasks. Three millennials I interviewed emphasized how their managers did not share information with them; as a result, they felt unable to connect with their managers and with their jobs themselves. If the employee does not understand the objective of a task, it will be hard for them to produce good results. It will also make it hard for the young employee to learn and gain confidence. This brings poor results to the organization. The young employee becomes more of a robot than a thinker.

All a manager needs to do is to explain a task—in person, by email, or by phone—and let the employee feel that the manager trusts them enough to take them into his or her confidence. I once had a manager who would make me feel stupid when I went to her with questions. She would make faces and body movements as if calling me a "moron." I avoided going to her with questions unless I absolutely had to. Instead, I would go to other employees who had worked there longer, in hopes that they would help me. However, I realized that a few coworkers were negatively competitive and would talk behind my back. Sometimes, I benefited when my boss discovered that I was afraid of going to her and preferred to go to someone else. This realization occasionally provoked the boss into coming to me and providing me with more precise instructions on the task.

Managers need to hold scheduled staff meetings with a shared agenda so staff also come prepared with updates. Managers need to run the meetings with a positive attitude to encourage staff to express their opinions freely and not feel scared of saying something stupid. I also encourage managers to hold one-on-one meetings with their staff—even monthly or quarterly—for guidance and mentoring.

Always deliver feedback constructively. Millennials should take advantage of constructive criticism, even if it reflects one's weakness, because that is the only way to learn and grow professionally. If a person closes their mind and is overly sensitive about feedback, they will never learn. Managers may not want to invest in an employee if she or he feels the employee takes feedback too sensitively. Millennials should always keep their minds open.

## Hiring system

Organizations and companies need to work seriously on their hiring systems. Firstly, and most importantly, a company must identify its needs and the assets that will benefit the team and organization. Next, the company must decide on the job description and the level of experience needed. Would an interim position fill the gap, or would mid-level experience be better? The company should set interview questions based on the position they decide, not a generic set of questions. However, it is not only about expertise. Personality questions also play a significant role. A company can always train staff on skills, but it is hard to change attitudes.

Sometimes, in interviews, people may be nervous and unable to express themselves well, but it is obvious they have the experience and skills for the position. That is why I believe before the interview starts officially, interviewers should chat with prospective employees in a friendly manner to make them comfortable before throwing questions at them. Young employees do not have enough experience in interviews. Employers need to go easy on them and ask them questions related to an analytical way of thinking and not just experience. They are not experienced, and the position is an interim one, so why would anyone ask them the same questions they would ask someone who has ten years of experience and evaluate the interview based on that?

By using this hiring method, companies bring unqualified people into an interim position. That person ends up being unchallenged and bored. Eventually, the new employee quits in less than a year. No wonder certain companies have a high turnover of staff. The interview process is time-consuming and costly. To figure out hiring needs, put them in a post, collect and screen resumes, do initial interviews, do second and final interviews, select the right candidate, and have HR work on the offer requires considerable time, effort, and money. Dealing with orientation and familiarizing the new employee with the work also takes time and energy. The process sometimes can take up to one to two months until a new employee is hired.

Imagine going through all that, and in a short time, that person quits the job. There are better ways to go about interviews from the start. One of the better ways for organizations to hire is to select the right staff to conduct the interview. The interview should involve a committee of staff members who are familiar with the needs of the position and will be working with the position. For example, in one of my jobs, the company's vice president was interviewing candidates on her own for an interim position. She excluded staff from the interview process, even though they would be working directly with the new person. She didn't know the exact type of person her team needed for the position and, as a result, ended up selecting a person who was overqualified for an interim position. The person did not last six months before getting bored by the lack of challenge and quitting.

When companies are hiring for a management position, they should hire candidates based on their extensive experience in the needed area.

However, I have noticed that this is not always the criterion companies use to decide. Sometimes, the hiring system is not very professional, and an interviewer might end up being impressed by a candidate for personal reasons rather than for professional ones.

## Staff Capacity

Companies are responsible for training and developing managers' skills regularly. Not all trainings are costly (actually, some are free). But even if they are expensive, the investment is worth every penny. Trainings are an investment in the organization as a whole, not just in an individual. What managers learn, they can teach to their staff, which has a positive impact on the overall environment.

At the same time, staff need skill development, regardless of their level. There are always people inside the organization who are good at something they can share with the whole organization in a monthly workshop or meeting. Call it capacity-building workshops, and do it in-house repeatedly.

Mike told me a story about a coworker who is an expert and holds a Ph.D. in the subject matter. He is a genius, but when it comes to implementing tasks, he is not a hard worker. Ask him a question, though, related to his specialty, and he is better than any consultant the company hires for the job. Yet no one utilized that skill in this genius and labeled him based on his achievements. Mike said, "*if they gave him the work they give consultants that cost them so much money, he would do it better and cheaper because he is already getting paid a salary.*" He is just not noticed in his capacity. Let that person hold a workshop for the staff to discuss matters related to the work they do and benefit them.

I also advise staff to invest in their self-development. They should keep working on skills they recognize as areas for improvement. I have taken many online courses on my own and that have not cost me much. One website I love is called Udemy. They have courses about everything; courses do not exceed $15, and customers have access to the course for life. Reading is another great way to grow. One doesn't have to buy the books; they can rent them from the library.

## Set Goals

It is crucial to set goals in one's life and one's profession. Employees should always ask themselves: what do I want to achieve from my career? They do not just want to be in a job to get paid, although salary is an important aspect. However, employees want to see themselves going somewhere with their career unless they want to stay where they are or keep changing jobs. Many people want to be promoted and reach a higher level. Some may want to have their own business at one point, but they want to gain experience first. Perhaps they want to go into a different field that might require taking different courses or attaining a degree. It helps to be aware and to have a goal. Even on a daily basis, it is good to know what the activities are that one needs to accomplish to go forward.

If a person wants to get promoted from program assistant to project manager, he or she needs to demonstrate specific skills, such as being able to multitask efficiently and on time. The person also needs to show that they take instructions well and work great with a team. They need to demonstrate that they are acquiring management and organizational skills, in addition to analytical thinking skills. Goals are incredible. They are the incentives a person can create for themselves to look forward to.

Even on a personal level, one should have goals. Getting married involves many steps before the wedding. It might be nice to travel or buy a house, and so on. We only attain goals with planning and hard work. Without a goal in mind, people scatter their energies and, in the end, remain unaccomplished. There are many resources on how to set goals including numerous courses, sessions, and mentors.

My children and I took many courses with Proctor Gallagher Institute including goal achieving and self-development. We started setting goals for our professional and personal lives. We even started doing a weekly call together to do "checks and balances" on our goals, so we were accountable to someone else. Sometimes, it helps to make a commitment to someone else. That way, when one updates them, he or she is excited to show the things he or she has done so far toward a goal. Other people can be useful as guides and can provide feedback so that the goal setter can move forward. Learn from others. If people lag on their goals, their commitment buddy will encourage them and give them a push to move forward instead of giving up.

I cannot express how many times I have reached a point where I thought I could no longer go on writing this book. I felt overwhelmed and lost at times. Sometimes I worried I would spend years of my life writing this book and doing nothing else. When I would take breaks from writing for a few days, I would struggle to go back. It was like taking a break from the gym for a while, but then dragging myself back on and off until, finally, I created a routine.

When I shared my struggle with Tarek, he immediately started guiding me. Right after our call ended, I could not stop writing. I don't know what I would have done if I did not get Tarek's support. It might have taken me much longer to get back to my goal. I advise people to find someone who thinks like them or is in favor of what they want to do, and be accountable to that person or persons.

Sometimes it helps to find a mentor. I have two main mentors in my life, for whom I am so grateful. Bob Proctor is the mentor I go to about my goals and achievements. Peggy McColl is my mentor when it comes to writing. Not only does she have a fantastic author's course, but she is a tremendous person whom one can reach out to directly to chat. She continues to inspire and guide me to go on with my book.

## Team Work

Successful managers, from a millennial perspective, are ones who treat them like coworkers and not inferiors. Millennials like to feel they are partners and that their opinion is valued; that's how Sandy puts it. Millennials also want managers who are able to recognize their weakness and work with them to help them develop. Sandy provided a good example. She told me she is so detail oriented that she forgets to see the big picture. One of her managers recognized the issue and worked with Sandy to overcome it. This made her happy, and she felt her manager cared about and was invested in her.

I love teamwork. Every workplace should promote a healthy, teamwork-oriented environment. Ideas flow in such a fantastic way when people think together—they can practically do magic. Teamwork is the solution to negative competition. Unfortunately, negative competition is one of the biggest issues in the workforce. Many have been taught not to share, so others don't become better at what they do than they are.

From my experience, I believe it is possible to work with anyone, from difficult people to negative people to arrogant people. It is all about individual workers, not about whom they are working with. If workers are confident to be at their best and do not care what others think of them or their ideas, they will be eventually seen. Workers can't just go with the majority. They need to go with what they believe in. If employees have an idea, but are not sure how the rest might see it, they mustn't be shy or afraid to share it. If they know how to phrase it correctly, coworkers will be able to see their perspective. If the idea isn't received well today, it might be later, or at least, the employee tried to put it out there. I have seen people in meetings listening to unreasonable ideas from senior management, which they know will not work. But they are not willing to present a counteroffer or even their perspective on why they think this idea might be challenging to implement. Instead, staff gossip and criticize the idea after the meeting, yet they go about implementing it.

Of course, the result is that they blame senior management for the idea when they are equally responsible. This is what teamwork is all about. We all work for the same cause, and believe in the mission of our work. No one is better than another; we complete each other. We each have our unique way of thinking that together can have an impact.

## Decision-Making & Transparency

Staff should be involved in the decision-making process. They understand the needs and challenges because they are affected by them. Managers should not hesitate to involve staff if they are stuck. Once a decision is made jointly, it becomes everyone's responsibility. However, if the decision is merely handed down from above, staff might not care the same way a manager would because they were not a part of the decision. Managers should not underestimate young staff, who have minds of their own and impressive ideas. They just need encouragement and to feel their opinion matters.

Managers and CEOs need to find creative ideas to take their company to new heights. Excluding staff from decision-making turns staff into machines. Most companies and organizations engage their staff in discussions about challenges. This is great.

When Amanda described her workplace, she told me that whenever an issue arises at work, senior management meets, discusses, and comes up with a solution that they impose on staff. She said, "*We really have better solutions, being the ones working on the project, so why do they exclude us from the thinking part?*" Amanda feels that management looks down on younger staff as if they do not know how to think analytically and need to be given solutions, rather than participating in their development. Exclusion causes staff to feel unworthy and untrustworthy. Amanda told me that she eventually lost her passion for her work. Now, she only does what she is asked, nothing more.

Sandy said, "*I like managers to be honest with me and not play games leaving me to figure out how they feel about me professionally.*"

Sandy feels there is a lack of transparency on her manager's end. She did not get feedback on their performance on a regular basis except maybe at the end of the year. I have worked in places where I went all year with no feedback. At the end of the year, in a performance review, my managers would tell me things that surprised me. I'd wonder why they hadn't communicated this to me earlier, when I could have fixed it.

Sandy thinks that a lot of managers are so caught up with proving themselves and making themselves stand out in front of *their* managers that they forget to manage those below them. Another issue is that some managers are hired from outside the organization and lack an insider's understanding of the organization's work and tasks.

Managers come from different experiences and backgrounds, so sometimes communicating with them can be challenging. I once was assigned to a manager who had no prior hands-on experience with what we were doing. Instead of her supporting me, I ended up mentoring and training her. With time, it became frustrating and time-consuming. I gave up attempting to figure out things on my own and reporting to her rather than asking for her advice. Despite that, I was able to have an experience that allowed me to be independent, which makes me privileged.

## Incompetent Managers

It is challenging to imagine that an organization would hire an incompetent manager; one might think an employee is exaggerating if they say their boss is incompetent. Maggie had an awful manager on her first job. She said her manager's office was right next to where she sat. He would call her to come to his office to staple a paper for him. Most of the tasks he gave her were hideous. She was the longest to stick around in that job, which was four months. Most employees who had preceded her quit within weeks. When she left, her manager's boss called her and said: "*Tell me what is it that keeps driving the staff out of this office.*" She told him honestly what was going on. She had no respect for a boss who treated his employees by disrespecting their skills and time. It seemed that the higher authorities had had no idea about what was going on; not only was the manager incompetent, but his manager was too. It doesn't take a genius to realize there is an issue if employees routinely quit after a just few weeks from hire.

Dena once had a boss who was in her early '50s, and could not do anything on a computer but type. If Dena's boss wanted to save a file, find a document, or do anything on the computer, she would continue to come to Dena to do it for her. This woman had been the director of the organization for three years and had worked in high positions for many years. I have no idea how she got away with her technological illiteracy and made it that far in a position.

Ula worked at a large nonprofit for two years. She was happy and learning well, but the workload was too much for her. For some reason, she convinced herself it was time to move on to another job although she could have worked out the workload with her manager, whom she got along well with. She accepted the first job offer she received. One of the factors that encouraged her to accept was the salary. Ula has now been at her job for four years, and she swears that she has barely worked. Her job is flexible. She can work from home three to four days a week, and when she is in the office, she sits behind her desk with barely any work. At first, she thought it was a temporary situation because her boss traveled often. After a year of requesting work, and trying to keep herself busy, she started to become frustrated. She tried to enjoy the easy job and good salary for another year until she realized she was not learning or developing any skills. Eventually, her boss was fired, and she was hopeful that now a new manager would come, and she would have work. However, her new manager managed her remotely from another state; she would give Ula some work on and off, but nothing of consequence.

After three years, Ula started applying for jobs elsewhere, but did not get good offers. She is still working at her organization while applying for jobs, but she told me she has lost her confidence and is concerned about getting a real job where people actually work. Ula works for a huge organization that receives lots of funding. What is going on? Who monitors the work and the results? I could not believe her story. If I had not known her personally, I would have thought her story was exaggerated.

I have not for the life of me been able to figure out how there are so many incompetent people in leading roles. I swear I even saw them getting promoted. I had to reconsider my understanding for a promotion if it was about achievements, abilities, or incompetence. Can you imagine the damage to the staff's morale when they see an incompetent person being promoted and rewarded? I am talking about incompetence, and I have proof of mistakes, errors, and weaknesses that the younger staff had to fix. I guess, when a manager delegates his or her work to younger staff and gets the credit for the results, this can be deceiving to upper management because they only look at results.

Yet, in every place I worked or heard about from friends, there was at least one person on a higher level who was unequipped for the position but got away with it. One of my coworkers was highly qualified and brilliant at her work. She was from the older millennial generation. She got promoted rapidly, but she truly earned it. Management-wise, she sucked because she was good and the actual work but not as a manager. That would have been fine if she were provided with training to develop those skills.

The issue was more than that. Her manager, a senior director, was so incompetent that he would delegate all of his work to her. In addition to her own work and managing a team, she also had to do her manager's job. It was difficult for her to focus on her team; from being a subject matter expert, she became a lousy manager whom the majority of staff hated, and she became frustrated with her job. She found out that all the work she had done for her boss had not been acknowledged. He took all the credit and praise. One day, the company gave her boss an award for his achievements, accompanied by an attractive bonus. Eventually, my coworker quit her job because she could not deal with the situation anymore. Her boss is not only still around, but got promoted again recently. Good employees are a significant loss for companies when companies fail to acknowledge them and put them in the right department.

This is why it is important for a candidate to do due diligence about the place they are considering working for. If they end up working in a place where they are unhappy, they should leave as soon as possible.

## Just Say Thank You

Everyone loves to feel appreciated on a personal and professional level. Kind words make a person feel rewarded. Sometimes managers only point out employees' faults and overlook the good. Just because good results are expected and employers should strive to attain them, all employees are not equally accomplished. Some employees work harder than others. Acknowledging them not only makes them want to give more, but sets a good example and offers incentive for those who are not putting in enough effort.

I once asked one of my managers why she doesn't give her employees positive feedback when they do a good job. Her response was *"They are doing their job, which is what they were hired to do. Why thank them?"* Millennials' request of their managers is as simple as: *"Just say thank you."* They want to feel they are appreciated and valued when they do a good job. They are also open to feedback to improve.

## Delegate Work

Everyone should be busy at work. However, there are times when there might be more going on than usual or there might be more deadlines to meet than usual; this can be stressful. Some employees have more work than others; delegating work allows staff to do their jobs to the best of their abilities and become more independent, rather than feeling watched. Sandy said, *"We need autonomy at jobs rather than being told how to do every step and be watched."*

Managers delegate work to their staff based on ability and strength. In an article published by Brian Tracy International, the author says, *"Delegation is one of the most important and effective management skills. Without the ability to delegate effectively, it is impossible for you to advance in management to higher positions of responsibility."*

Delegating is a critical ability from a managerial point of view, because managers have to work with employees to develop goals and achieve the organization's incentives. This works by individually assigning each person the work they have been hired to do. The key is to communicate the task to the right person. In this way, the manager is able to at least hold a single person accountable for the progress and completion of the task, instead of blaming it on a team in which half of the people have no idea what's going on. Delegating is beneficial to the "manager-employee" relationship because delegating work to the right person requires prior assessment of all employees' skills and areas of expertise.

# Fight for Your Team

One millennial asked me, "*When your boss is weak and insecure and is not willing to fight for you, can you fight for yourself?*" My response was: "*I'm sure you can, but before you proceed with the fight, prepare well and study your strategies well. You need to understand and be accountable for the consequences. In war, you either win, or you lose, but in the end, you gave your best and learned for future fights.*" I remember when my son had difficulties with one of his managers about meeting deadlines over quality. He was concerned that by being pressured with a timeline, he would not be able to put out the highest quality work. His manager wanted him to meet deadlines, regardless of the quality. He wanted to fix the issues and provide a high-quality product even if it was late. He discussed the situation with me because he was having ethical problems with it. This was a tricky situation. Of course, quality is essential, but at the same time, if a customer is expecting the delivery on time, and there is a delay, that might affect the purchase.

On the other hand, if a consumer receives a defective product, the customer might become upset and he might never want to buy from that company again. This is a manager's call at the end of the day, and I told my son he should not fight it that much. He should clearly state his position and document it in an email, but meet the deadline as the manager requested.

Millennials are unsure how to stand up for themselves in certain situations due to their lack of experience and fear of authority. But a good manager is willing to stand up for and protect her team.

Millennials like to feel that their manager is strong enough to fight for them when needed. Amanda told me that the president of her organization once blamed her for something she did not do. Amanda's boss often made hasty choices that Amanda did not support. Once, her boss made a decision that Amanda thought was wrong; Amanda stated her position and told her boss why she disagreed, but ultimately went ahead and did as she was asked. The president of the organization was not happy with this decision and wrongly assumed that Amanda had made it when, in fact, her boss had made the decision. When the president criticized Amanda, Amanda's boss never took responsibility for her actions and let the president think that it was Amanda's decision. Essentially, Amanda's boss threw her under the bus and made her look guilty. First, when managers do this, they are teaching their staff unethical behaviors. Second, their teams will not respect them as managers. Third, it is cowardly to be afraid to be held accountable, yet to jump on the staff the moment any team member makes a mistake.

## Find Solutions, Not Blame

One piece of advice I give to my children and young coworkers is, "*Stop looking around for someone to blame and look for solutions.*" Blaming others never solves a problem; on the contrary, it complicates matters. There is always a solution to a problem if you think hard enough. Unfortunately, in the work environment, people often find it easy to blame coworkers or higher management for everything. They spend hours and days convincing themselves that the issue lies somewhere else, not with them. I believe that examining problems objectively without judging enables managers to see a way out. I also think the time put into analyzing the problem and discovering who is to blame for it could be better spent figuring out a way out of it. Learn from it, and don't repeat it.

I had a job that I found difficult. It was beyond my experience. Millennials were doing the work much better than I was. I felt crappy and started blaming it on the way I was raised, on my divorce, and on the workplace for not providing me with enough guidance. After a year, I realized that I was screwing over my career, and I needed to face my faults and work on them. I listed my weaknesses on a piece of paper and asked myself, "*What do I need to do to turn those weaknesses into strengths?*" I started Googling free courses on how to write efficiently and turn my weaknesses into strengths. In a year, I saw significant improvement. After I improved my shortcomings, I gained more confidence in my skills, and I got promoted. Then, I started coaching young employees and sharing tips I have learned along the way. Within five years, I knew I wanted to be a coach for millennials because I see and believe in their potential and understand them.

## Corporate Culture

One person can change a negative work environment. One should never accept an environment where they are unhappy by isolating themselves from everyone else, discouraging themselves, or following the crowd. One person can bring something good into an old culture and make it better. If people only realized how many hours a week they spend with coworkers, they would understand that they spend more time with those people than with friends and family. A person cannot be in the same place for years, put in long hours, and be miserable each day. It will kill you: emotionally, psychologically, and professionally. I once went to an organization where people sat in their offices and worked all day without talking to each other or doing any activities together. I'm not saying people go to work to socialize, but it is a healthy thing to chat with coworkers during breaks and get to know one another as humans. Coworkers have a lot to share and learn from. Talking to colleagues builds bonds and creates a friendlier environment. Look at Google's building—how energetic and inspiring it is. Why would Google create such comfort for their staff if they only want them to get the work done? Because they understand the importance of a healthy work environment. The happier an employee is at work, the more productive they are.

If a person wakes up in the morning dreading the day because they have to go to work, there is something definitely wrong with them, the place they are working at or both. My son moved to Richmond to be close to his girlfriend. He accepted a job thinking it was the best fit for him. He thought, "*How bad could it be? I will gain experience even if for a year and settle in Richmond until I find a better a job.*" He did not even last three months in his new job. The environment was so toxic and dysfunctional that he either had to accept it as it was, which was hard for him to do, or try to find a way to fit in, but it was too difficult for him. He chose to quit, and I supported him.

What I am trying to say is this: if a person is unable to fit into a workplace, regardless of the reason, and if they cannot create enough positive change to survive there, quitting may be an option. However, I suggest people try to find a solution first and view quitting as a last resort. For example, it took me a year in one of my jobs to get to know most of my colleagues because they were not social. Eventually, I started talking to them in the kitchen, in the restroom, and before staff meetings. I started expressing my opinions about the culture and suggesting some changes. With time, I realized that people were nice. They just want to fit into a culture immediately instead of trying to be themselves.

If a person decides that they have to leave their job because it has become intolerable, they should draw up a budget before they quit and look around for other employment opportunities. They should protect themselves so that they can make that car payment or pay off their student loan, and make sure that they are not short on rent every month because they left their job prematurely.

There are ways in which one can get a sense of a company's work environment before accepting a job there. A website called Glassdoor posts reviews of different companies that are shared by current and past employees of those companies.

One approach a person can take if something is bothering them about work is to sit down with management and address their concerns. Even if management does not take action the first time broaching the topic, at least the person knows their input is on file in case someone else raises similar complaints. Also, sometimes upper management looks at exit interviews and complaints, particularly if there is an investigation. Of course, if one goes to HR and they do nothing, one should go back again and see if anything has changed. Take notes even if HR says something verbally.

In general, HR does their jobs, and most of the time, they follow up. A person can seek advice from coworkers or friends with knowledge of what to do in similar situations. Online platforms also have a lot of resources on what to do if HR ignores a complaint.

I read an article on *Business Insider* about this topic. The article provided the example of Susan F. Fowler, an employee at Uber who alleged sexual harassment in the workplace. Her allegations were ignored, so she posted a blog that got the attention of the tech company, which launched an internal investigation. According to the *Business Insider* article, Fowler wrote in the post, "Fowler claimed that Uber's HR department was part of the problem. She wrote that Uber covered up for "high performers" and failed to take actions against instances of gender bias in the office."

The article emphasizes that the first step is to file a claim with HR, and give them a chance to address the complaint and fix the problem. Another suggestion in the article is, "If HR has made it clear that they don't have your back, it's time to start looking for support elsewhere. Fried recommends alerting the U.S. Equal Employment Opportunity Commission."

The bottom line, as Richard Branson puts it, is: "*Clients do not come first. Employees come first. If you take care of your employees, they will take care of the clients.*"

# Workload

Millennials are hardworking and ambitious. They are skilled and believe they should get promoted quickly. They work long hours to prove themselves and get ahead competing with their peers. Sandy elaborated on this point by saying that once she became confident about herself and the work, she got promoted. That is when she stopped working long hours. So it seems the objective of doing hard work was the payoff of a promotion. It might sound negative, but I understand Sandy's point. Once people prove themselves and are acknowledged, then they don't have to worry because it will take at least three or more years before another promotion is on the table. There might not be another promotion at one's current job, so in this situation, Sandy would have had to seek an external opportunity. This is what she ended up doing. After she got promoted twice in two years, she wanted to get promoted again after a short while. She knew that would not happen at her job, so she went for another job.

I don't think promotions are necessarily related to the amount of work one does in a short time. There are other skills that one needs to prove in order to go higher in the company. It also depends on the size of the workplace and if there is room to grow further. Some organizations are too small to have higher openings. Others have too high competition.

Managers' role is to work with their young staff on time management and prioritization. Sometimes millennials lack time management skills and think the workload is the problem. I once witnessed a situation between a millennial and her director, who called her into his office to ask her why she worked around twelve hours of overtime, and sometimes more, according to her timesheet. He told her if she was overworked, she needed to address it with her direct supervisor, or delegate some of the work to interns and assistants.

Nadine did not understand that the manager was trying to help her. She took it personally that he was questioning her honesty in charging for extra time on her timesheet. At first, I felt bad for her and thought of what a jerk the director was. Nadine chose to quit her job immediately and gave her two weeks' notice. A few days later, I saw her director in the kitchen. He said to me, "*I am really surprised that Nadine submitted her resignation.*" He explained that he felt Nadine lacked time management skills and the ability to prioritize, and wanted her to work normal hours for her own sake. I told him he should sit with her again and explain that. He did, but Nadine insisted on believing what she had understood from him the first time and she took another job.

I met Nadine a few times for lunch after she quit her job, and she told me how her manager at her new job recommended that she attend time management classes. She felt that Nadine was working unnecessarily long hours. Again, Nadine was upset by the feedback, but it was too early to quit that job too. I spoke with Nadine frankly and asked her if both managers were wrong. I also asked her if her job paid for her to take time management classes, what would she have to lose? She eventually did take classes, and stopped complaining.

If workload is a result of a work system that is not handled well by the managers, they should address that. Employees, especially younger ones, are afraid to complain about the workload because they don't want to look incapable of doing their work. Managers need to put themselves in their employees' shoes and decide if the workload is doable or not.

Unfortunately, Americans are rated as one of the highest in the world in terms of the number of hours they work. Some say this could be due to lack of time management abilities or an overwhelming workload, but I genuinely believe it gets back to management's competence and skills. Ula told me, "*The problem with our workload is that our managers are overworked too, and they have no time to notice us. Actually, they try to dump some of their work on us thinking we are not doing enough.*" So, we have a chain of stressful commands coming from top to bottom. The ones who pay the highest price are the ones who are skilled and great at their jobs.

One of the big problems that organizations have, which also reflects on the heavy workload of staff, is the abundance of long, unnecessary meetings. If staff attends at least one to two meetings a day, there goes at least two hours of their time. I'm being modest, assuming each meeting might take just one hour, but I have seen them drag on much longer. By the time the meetings is over, there are so many more emails to respond to in addition to the work that was planned for the day. Another issue I have encountered is that work-related travel piles extra work on a person. There are employees whose job requires them to travel often. A person needs to prepare for the trip, do the work they need to do before they leave, and then, while traveling, do the work they are going for and the work they left behind.

The trips can become stressful, and when the person returns to the office, so much work is waiting for in addition to the work they brought back from the trip. I hate the trip reports that take forever to write, but no one ends up reading. I swear I had a manager who, instead of reading my recommendations from the trip, which I believe were useful, she would spend time editing my report that was solely for her to read. Most of the time, she ended up not reading the report because she forgot the reason that I gave it to her in the first place.

## Why Should I Go to Work?

*Train people well enough so they can leave.*
*Treat them well enough so they don't want to.*

*~ Richard Branson*

I asked myself that question for more than thirty years, and yet I kept doing it. I'm sure a lot of people ask themselves this question. Some keep going on, like me, and others just figure the answer out on their own and move on. I asked millennials what motivates them to go to work each day, and got good answers. I realized that they thought about the question closely and had a clear understanding of it. This confirms that millennials are more cognizant of themselves and their needs than previous generations.

Very few millennials I interviewed said that they got personal gratification from working. Sandy said, "*The previous generation cared more about the stability that came with work whereas millennials, we care about the personal gratification that comes from work. We believe in adding impact.*" People make a change because they are unhappy. No one leaves a job because they are thrilled to be there.

Some people say they like their colleagues and the work environment. Others say they learn and gain experience to find better jobs. The majority of people go to work because they want to pay their debts and earn enough income to live a decent financial life.

People often talk about how millennials quit their jobs within a short time period. An average millennial will change three to four jobs in their short professional life span. One often hears senior management saying that millennials do not stick to one position for long. I believe that is true. So do millennials; they admit it. Few care to think of the reason millennials quit jobs so soon. That is why millennials became the joke of the century.

I wanted to understand millennials' reasoning, so I asked my young former coworkers who had quit their jobs why they left. Mike had this to say: "*1. Growing and equality 2. Wages 3. We see what a good life looks like, unlike the previous generations. I want to live this good life but cannot afford it. I move for a job that pays better. 4. People make changes because they are unhappy. The older generation, due to their age and experience, are holding high positions, and they are comfortable waiting for retirement. They do not understand what we are going through. We see through social media that our friends and others have better jobs, and we want to move forward like them.*"

I have worked with two different types of millennials. The first type changes jobs fast, and the other type sticks to their job without being motivated. However, both types want to be recognized by their managers and rewarded, mostly financially. They understand that the higher the position goes, the higher the salary goes, and they aim for the promotion even if they are still weak in experience. In addition, millennials lose their motivation at the job quickly—most of the time in less than a year. I believe millennials make a decision to change or stay based on their peers' decisions. If the turnover is high at work, they tend to follow the crowd, particularly their peers in the same work environment.

At one of my jobs, there were many short deadlines, but not much room for growth. There was also an absence of management feedback.

Young employees do their jobs until they are bored and unchallenged. They expect after a year of proving their skills, they will get promoted, but when they apply for a higher position, they are unsuccessful and do not receive clear feedback. They are left to wonder if they are unappreciated or unrecognized and choose to look for another job opportunity. They assume a different job will have better opportunities, when in reality it could be the same.

The second type of staff stayed longer at their job even though there wasn't much room for growth, mostly because the organization was small. Yet there wasn't any peer pressure or influence to leave, so they adjusted to the norm. They were unmotivated and not learning enough skills to take them anywhere better. Consequently, they started losing their confidence.

These days, companies and organizations look at a candidate's years of experience and how often they have been promoted throughout the years. So if a person sticks with the same title for more than five years, the chances of getting a job become harder. Eventually, a person is competing with the younger generation who just graduated and is willing to do the same job for less money.

Most millennials I have worked with, known, interviewed, or even raised tell me that changing jobs after two years is reasonable. It allows them to have different experiences, helps them figure out what type of work they desire, and allows them to grow and develop into higher positions.

Millennials lack challenge at their jobs; they are lost and do not know what they want. This may sound like an attack on millennials, but these are their words, not mine. They have good reasons to leave, but they do not necessarily go about it the right way. Here are some reasons millennials mentioned as to why they quit their jobs:

### 1. Managers and management system:

Millennials tend to leave their jobs mostly because they are unhappy with their managers. They do not feel their managers understand and support them. They do not receive good mentoring and guidance to help them understand the work better to feel they are on the right track. They find themselves struggling to prove themselves and are left wondering if they are meeting the job requirements and whether their manager is satisfied with their work or not. Millennials feel that whether they work hard or not, they will get the same reaction from their managers: no feedback. They see some of their peers not putting in the same effort as they are, yet they both get paid to do the same work.

Often, millennials do not feel their managers communicate well with them, and they are left wondering if the problem is within them, not understanding the work, and they start losing confidence. Millennials do not have the skills to face their managers and request feedback, so they quit their jobs in the hope that another work environment will be better in terms of management. I blame the managers who do not invest in their team and provide feedback to help them grow. However, millennials have a responsibility to talk to the manager and get a response even if it is a negative one.

For example, if a manager is willing to sit with an employee and share areas that person needs to work on, that feedback might help that individual develop his or her skills. I know employees are frustrated about why the managers don't share this feedback before employees went to them. That is their role, and they should do that.

Maggie is in her early '30s, and when I asked her about her opinion, as a millennial and as a manager on this issue, she stated the following: *"There is good and bad for millennials changing jobs. Being young in experience does not always allow the person to make the right judgment of a management style and skills because they do not have a previous one to compare it with."* Maggie understood after she left her first job that she had the best managers but did not realize it until two years later when she had other experiences to compare it with. Looking back, Maggie said, *"They were very hands-off unless I needed their support. They gave me freedom of my time and projects. I am terrible at getting up in the morning, and they never cared what time I came in because they saw that I am good at getting the job done and they do not need to manage me in petty things that do not affect the work. That is the kind of manager I want to be. When I became a manager, I decided I was going to implement this style by training my team well and then giving them the freedom to do their work on their own."* Maggie believes that it takes about a year to figure out your manager.

### 2. Promotion:

Some millennials quit their jobs because they did not get the promotion they believed they earned. Millennials are eager for a promotion. They see it as a reward and acknowledgment for their hard work. Part of the management system is to have a system in-house that rewards those who are doing great by promoting them. Managers need to prepare their staff for a promotion by working with them on goals to achieve that level. However, this does not always happen, and all of a sudden, a millennial applies for a promotion and gets rejected. Most of the time, they are not given reasons why they were declined this opportunity. They are left wondering about the reasons, and sometimes this makes them feel that they are not appreciated. Also someone else might get promoted, who they do not necessarily believe is doing better work than them. This is indeed a poor management system. If managers do not feel their employees are ready for promotion because they still lack management skills, managers should sit with them and provide them feedback. Guide them on what they need to do to reach that level. Maybe suggest a course, or give them some tasks to manage interns to learn how to manage others. As Gandhi once said, *"Be the change that you wish to see in the world."*

### 3. Lack Challenge:

*"We lack challenge and get bored,"* Mike said to me. Doing the same

work over and over tends to be boring and unchallenging for millennials. Sometimes, this lack of challenge is what makes millennials want to go for a promotion hoping they will be doing more challenging work. Another option is to change jobs where they will be doing something different and more stimulating. Tarek told me how, at his first job, he was learning a lot, but after a year, it became repetitive. He could do it with his eyes closed. He wondered how so many baby boomers at his job had been doing the same work over and over for more than twenty years, and they never thought of changing jobs. Interesting how millennials see the older generation in that respect. The older generation believes that millennials are wrong to change positions quickly while millennials see previous generations as strange for sticking with a job for that long.

Tarek said, *"When we set at a job, all we do is run in repetition. We do not think outside the box at work, and we do not make decisions. We keep doing the same thing over and over again until we get bored and stop being challenged."*

### 4. Salary:

Most millennials live day to day from the income they earn. They carry one or more student loans. Sometimes, these loans can eat up $500-$800 monthly from a salary that could be up to $3,000 monthly. In addition to student loans, some millennials might have a car loan that is needed to commute to work. Of course, there are rent and other expenses on their salaries, which is inadequate for them to live a decent financial life without stressing about it. They tend to jump from one job to another in the hopes of getting paid better.

### 5. Flexibility:

Millennials love work-life balance. Teleworking at least once a week means the world to them. The number of vacation days annually matters more to millennials than previous generations. Many times, they leave a job that does not have such incentives to go to a place that does.

In conclusion, millennials tend to prefer startup businesses or self-employment. Some of them take the risk of joining a small startup because they believe they can learn more from scratch about how to start up a business and grow with it. In addition, a startup business allows creativity and flexibility to flow freely. They come up with ideas, test them, and go for it. They learn from their mistakes and move on to improve. Most startup business nowadays are ideas that millennials came up with and took the chance to start that idea and test it. Some of these ideas grew and became big corporations.

Social media and online businesses are becoming a big hit. Millennials come up with creative ideas and open an online business that does not cost them much but promises growth. At least, if the idea didn't grow, they have learned skills that they can take to their next job. Marketing an online business is a challenge and requires thorough study. For millennials, it is both easy and hard to avail themselves of online services for boosting businesses. Since more and more people shift toward starting their online market, the competition makes it harder for millennials to stand out in this aspect as well. Having an online business requires a lot of perpetual planning and risky decisions. More than 90 percent of all startup business fails because they couldn't find the right market to make it big.

However, it is not about the market at all but more about perseverance and identifying the right opportunities. Since millennials are very social, they have a good chance of hitting that mark in the startup business, and they feel they do not need to stick to a job to learn to stand up on their own.

If you have to quit your job, quit and don't look back. But before you do, make sure you know where you are going. The new place should be better and take you toward your dream job. If it is not your dream job, don't quit and accept a job just because you want to get the heck out of that depressing, stressful place. I can tell you so many stories of young coworkers who quit their jobs because they were miserable and landed in a more miserable one. One of my friends and coworkers, who is a millennial, was extremely good at what she did. I could see that she would be getting promoted soon, and she would do even better at her new position, but I had no idea why she was so miserable at her job. Even then she decided to accept the only job offer she got. She has been stuck in her new position for three years now and not only is she more miserable than she was at her old job, but she ended up losing her confidence and skills. Her new job was so complicated and corrupt that she would sit all day with nothing to do. There was nothing or anyone to learn from and no skills to develop. She is still young and needs to build skills and a career.

When one has wasted three years of their career n in an unsuitable place, it is hard to go ahead. She has been applying for jobs for two years now, but unfortunately has not been successful. The offers she got were either not up to her standards, or the working environment wasn't up to the mark. Today she is unsure of what type of jobs she is good at. I chatted with her a number of times and told her to take advantage of the time she has and take courses to develop her skills. Also, I advised her to volunteer and be active in networking. This is just one example, but I know of many who suffer in the same situation. Make sure when you are looking to move on to another job, you put your frustration aside, and look for what you love to do and where you want to be rather than focus on "I just want to get out of here." Change is good, but always choose better change.

Also, before you leave your job, go for the exit interview. Most work-places conduct an exit interview with the resigned employee. If there is HR, they will do the exit interview. Otherwise, the head of the organization will do it. Of course, there are few small organizations that do not do it, due to short capacity and maybe lack of interest. The objective of the exit interview is to help HR and the organization to understand the reasons behind the turnover of staff. Bosses file and document the interview if anyone from upper management is ever interested in understanding the reasons and improving the work conditions to decrease the number of people leaving the company without explanation.

However, from my experience in working in a number of places, and from what I heard from other colleagues in high positions, most of the time, the exit interviews are filed and not seen. Even HR does not necessarily take the time to review a trend, common reasons, or to even pay manage-ment's attention to the complaints or comments. However, that does not mean a person should not do it. One day, someone will care and review especially when the turnover becomes high.

I used to work in a sizeable nonprofit organization, and the turnover of staff was so high that annually about ten to fifteen people from a total of 150 employees would quit. The HR would conduct the exit interview and file it. It was apparent they didn't do much with the results they collected. When a new CEO got hired, the first thing he did was look into the exit interviews to understand the high turnover of staff. He hired an external consultant who started reviewing the exit interviews and came up with a report of the common reasons that led to many employees giving up on their jobs. He took the comments seriously and started cleaning up the organization. He fired a number of senior managers, placed managers in different departments where they were a better fit, and he dismissed people from the staff who had bad annual reviews.

There is a TV show called *Undercover Boss* where the manager of a huge company such as Burger King wears a disguise and goes to work at a low-level job in one of his or her many outlets. Nobody has any idea that this is the owner of the company. It allows the owner to see what goes on, on the ground level, i.e., how does the cashier feel about her job? What about the dishwasher or the person who hands the burgers to customers from the car window? *Undercover Boss* gets people to trust him because they think he's just like them and then afterward, he uses all this constructive criticism to reshape the company.

I encourage millennials to go through the exit interview before they leave. After all, unlike their parents, millennials have grown up in a world where they must rate and review everybody from their doctor to their Uber driver to their last purchase on Amazon. They will feel good by verbalizing their complaints about the workforce, and might do good for their colleagues who will struggle at work for the same reasons they did. Having testimonies about people's individual job experience on record is important. Millennials should prepare well for the exit interview and jot down in a professional manner the things that need improvement in the company, which provoked their leaving. Millennial employees can even raise these points as recommendations instead of criticism. This will sound professional, and hopefully, they will be heard.

One day at one of my jobs, a young man was so upset by his manager that he left on bad terms. In the exit interview, he spoke in an angry manner and unprofessionally by attacking people by name and making it personal. Ironically, this guy ended up leaving for another job that seemingly was better, and on his first day, he was informed that they changed their mind and preferred to postpone the opening for his position for six months. He got screwed and ended up without work for a while. Even if going back to his previous job temporarily had been an option, now it was not. If he wanted to apply for jobs and needed a recommendation, this made it complicated. It is good to leave professionally and with respect.

We must learn from experience, and when one moves to a new job, apply what he or she has learned. One does not want to keep changing jobs for the same reasons. What is it that would keep someone at the same job for a few years until he or she accumulates a good amount of experience and reach a higher position? It takes time, and one should not rush into going up the ladder so fast. It gets tiring and stressful. The higher one is in a position, the more responsibilities that individual will have, which might not be exactly where he or she had wanted to go. It isn't just about the salary and prestige of a position. Employees also want to do well and prove themselves. They do not want to reach a point where they are no longer confident in their skills. Once one is up, it is hard to go down. No one wants to get demoted after being promoted. At the same time, people don't want to get stuck in the same position for long if they end up struggling. The promotion gets harder then.

# CHAPTER 9
## *Learn from Millennials*

*"Learn to light a candle in the darkest moments of someone's life. Be the light that helps others see; it is what gives life its deepest significance."*

~ Roy T. Bennett

There is so much to learn from millennials and mostly for millennials to learn from each other. I asked a few millennials what advice they would like to give to the next generation. How can they help the next generation, who will grow up knowing technology and might still be facing rapid cultural changes during their time? Also, how can they inspire the next generation to continue developing the path they paved for them? What changes should they make so their time on this earth is better? Mona had this to say to the younger generation, *"I would cuddle them much less. I will make them do a lot more for themselves. Get jobs early on in restaurants and retail to test the waters with different internships."*

Here is some advice from millennials to Generation Z:

## Travel

Travel when you are young and be exposed to other cultures. If you get the chance to study abroad, do not waste the opportunity. You will learn so much and maybe come back home with a new language. Those experiences were life-changing for Sandy when she went to study in Egypt for a few months. She said, *"The experience shaped a lot of who I am."*

I met a number of millennials in my jobs who either studied abroad for a few months, or they did voluntary work for a year or so before they applied for jobs in the U.S. Their resumes looked good and they were more qualified for jobs than if they had not had that experience. In addition, they were good working with other clients from different countries. Your mind expands when you travel, and you become more open to other ideas and cultures. Traveling also makes you more of an independent person. You are on your own without family or friends' support. You will toughen up and learn how to make friends on your own. You will also learn how to take care of yourself by dealing with things as they come along. Some students go on an exchange program to another country and live with a family. This could be an exceptional experience to learn to deal with families other than your own.

I remember when I was in high school, a Norwegian girl came on an exchange program for one year to my school. Lill-Ann and I bonded so well that she became my best friend. She lived with an American family who were so extremely kind to her that I felt as if they were her real parents. They would invite me for Christmas and Thanksgiving dinners, and it felt like home to me. I wished her parents would adopt me. I learned so much from Lill-Ann, who was very active outdoors. We used to go hiking in the Rocky Mountains in Colorado where we lived. She also taught me how to ski because she skied a lot in Norway and was good at it. She even taught me how to swim professionally because she was on a swimming team at her school in Norway. I was lucky to meet her and learn from her because I did not get the chance to go abroad on an exchange program. Before I met Lill-Ann, I never knew much about Norway. Lill-Ann and I stayed in touch by snail mail for a few years. Then we lost touch. Until now… I wonder where she is and what she is doing. Imagine a friend like that—someone you never forget.

## Stand on Your Own Two Feet

Learn lots of skills while you are growing. They all come in handy and make you an independent person. You learn and grow so much when you are independent and rely on yourself. Parents' role is essential, and this does not mean you should be independent from your family physically and emotionally. On the contrary, you will grow closer and bond better with them. Sandy believes if a young person tries to live independently, although it may seem uncomfortable to move away, it will definitely shape you. Some millennials choose to study in the same town their parents live in, and they live at home for all or most of their college years. This is not necessarily bad but might keep you in your comfort zone and not provide you with the multi-cultural experience of being away. Sandy said: "*It will suck but distrust the discomfort. You will not even think twice about it in the end, and you will appreciate it.*"

## Make Uncomfortable Decisions:

This sounds scary, but it sure is true if you understand the meaning of it. When you make uncomfortable decisions, they are not dangerous or risky decisions, but rather they are decisions that will help you to grow by breaking your routine and doing things that may seem difficult and unusual at first. Even thinking about making a risky decision can be uncomfortable. There are so many books and motivational speakers who speak about this. My favorite is Bob Proctor who coaches on Paradigm Shift. A paradigm is our belief system: how we were programmed to think throughout our life. Paradigms are shaped by our upbringing, our circumstances, and the thoughts and philosophies we have developed from childhood. Often we live and view life through those belief systems that limit our growth and development. We can change our paradigm by introducing new ideas to replace the old ones. Shifting our paradigm leads to success.

One of the exercises the coaching program that I took with Proctor Gallagher Institute teaches people how to write with their non-dominant hand for ninety days. When I first started doing this, it was uncomfortable and frustrating. I didn't get the idea behind it. But I kept going because I felt Bob Proctor is a genius, and he was asking us to do something strange but not stupid. I kept doing it not only for ninety days but for a very long time.

Today, I write with my left hand as well as I do with my right hand. So, now I need a third hand to challenge because writing in my non-dominant hand became with time dominant, and I no longer find it awkward or uncomfortable. At one point, I injured my right hand and thought what the heck? I have my other hand to use. This is just one simple example of shifting your paradigm and getting yourself out of your comfort zone. It starts being difficult and frustrating, and then it becomes challenging until you feel comfortable. Significant changes in your life will teach you new skills and make you more experienced.

## Do Not Be Complacent

Sandy tells you, *"Don't sit and say, 'if it is not broken, don't fix it.' If it is not broken, that is great, but what can you do to insure that it will never break?"* Sandy's message is that one must always look for something else to make you stand out instead of being complacent and just settle. Always find a challenge, and try to chase after that. So many people stay in their unhappy job because they are terrified of leaving and fear of the unknown. What do they accomplish in the long run? Not much. Their life becomes a daily routine, unchallenging and boring. They become miserable without realizing that they are just one step away from the change they need to make to get them out of their misery. Just take the leap, and don't worry about falling.

## Make Time to Develop Others

While you are growing and developing, share your experiences and knowledge with others. You can help so many people grow and be an example. Sandy says, *"if you click with someone and can be their mentor, do it. It is not only going to help them, but it also will help you."* She gives an example of how she learned to understand herself better by mentoring and coaching others professionally. I went through this experience myself by mentoring and coaching millennials throughout my career and personal life, which is how I ended up writing this book. I would not have learned from my children and other millennials if I did not coach and mentor them. I heard directly from them their challenges and concerns, and I learned from them skills and creativity that I lacked.

## Have Multiple Sources of Income

If you are comfortable with a 9-5 job, that is fine but don't settle for the income from your job. Sandy tells you *"always have a side hustle."* She always looked for a side hobby to monetize. For example, she grew up dancing and was able to diversify her income from doing side jobs teaching others dancing. It might not generate a lot of income, but at least it is not a wasted hobby, and it can generate some extra income for you. Sandy was always able to plan for vacation trips from that extra money she created from dancing classes.

## Utilize Social Media Wisely

Learn from millennials' experience because they are the first generation to invent and use social media. Social media can be so useful if you use it right and wisely. Online businesses will be flourishing during your time; make smart decisions. Even education is turning into an online opportunity nowadays, and it will grow to be an alternative for in-class studying. You will be able to study, work, and run your online business at the same time. Learn the needed skills to make use of social media, and do not waste unnecessary time on it. Don't let social media take you away from socializing in person. It is so different to be with your peers to network, learn, and socialize rather than relying entirely on social media.

We, as parents of millennials, need to change our tactics by providing our children with life skills, so they excel as an innovative generation.

## Volunteer

Volunteering can help you see a new perspective on how you are not only part of the system when it benefits you. When you volunteer anywhere, whether it be through a professional platform or just on your own, it is essential to character building. It is good to take some time off from the usual social and professional life, and spend some time doing activities that don't *physically* provide you with anything but have a gigantic impact on your character. Volunteering is all about being ambitious in learning and, especially, being selfless. When you work for something which doesn't pay or benefit your career exclusively, it tends to open up an outlook on life that drives you to focus on things that matter to you instead of being dictated by factors like working hours, pay, management, peer pressure, work pressure and the list goes on.

# CHAPTER 10
## Parents of Millennials

*"It is not what you do for your children, but what you have taught them to do for themselves, that will make them successful human beings."*

~ Ann Landers

I tried to interview parents to hear their point of view as parents of millennials. I was truly surprised that the majority of parents I reached out to were not interested in being interviewed. The very few I interviewed were conservative in what they shared and how open they were to me in terms of responding to my questions. Whereas, all twelve millennials I reached out to interview responded positively. I think the millennial generation is more open and vocal and wants to be heard. They are not shy in expressing their opinion and seem to understand themselves well. I had no difficulty getting thorough responses. Whereas, the few parents that I interviewed mostly didn't have much to share or had difficulty being open. I believe, the idea of expressing their opinion in front of a stranger and talking about their own family made them more reserved. Of course, this may not be true for all millennials and their parents; it is simply what I observed in my interviews.

*T*he parents of most millennials are either baby boomers or the Generation Xers. There is no question that parents play the most significant role in molding their children's personality. Children learn and become conditioned about the habits that their parents embed in them throughout the years as they grow up. The parents of millennials grew up in a time of crime and high rate of divorced parents, so it is no surprise that they wanted to raise children to be safe and successful. A number of articles online show us parents as being overprotective and caring for our children, even when they are adults; they describe the millennial parents as "helicopter parents" as a reference to them hovering over their grown-up children to ensure they achieve a competitive advantage in their lives as well as their general wellbeing. I am not sure if I feel offended about this description. Being loving and caring, even protective, is a role parents should play. No matter how old your children are, you will always worry about them and hope they are safe. The truth is we live in a world where evil exists, and as parents, we worry about our children more than we worry about ourselves. However, if the loving and caring reach a point of spoiling our children and making them dependent and unable to succeed on their own, we should raise the red flag.

Parents of millennials learned from their experience and wanted to see their children have better opportunities than they did. They do not like to see their children stressing about finances because then their children will be making choices they do not necessarily have a passion for but rather because they need to survive. I wish that life had been easy on me and I had known that it was better to go after what I loved and not what is just required to secure a basic life. So, whatever I learned that I was unable to implement and do in my own life, I wanted to give to my children to help them save time and succeed while they were still young. I wanted them to do something good for themselves and others around them instead of just worrying about making ends meet. I don't see this as hovering around our children as much as supporting them as much as possible. My parents loved me, there is no doubt about that, but they did not teach me how to go after my passion. I was raised to go after whatever the norm was in those days. I had ambitions that were mixed with guilt, thinking if I went or even thought beyond the norm, I would be considered a rebellious child.

Daniel is a father of three millennial boys. He told me that he and his wife raised their children by spoon-feeding them each step along the way.

When I asked him why he thought they did that, he responded by saying, *"not sure, but I think that is how all parents around us were, and we felt we should follow the norm."* Obviously, Daniel and his wife never thought of what the best approach with their children was. Rather they wanted to fit in with other parents. He told me, *"I wish I knew what I know now; I would go back and teach my children how to think and come up with decisions on their own."*

I want my children to know they have choices and the most important decision is to do for a living what they love. That is when they will succeed. I supported both of my children in quitting their jobs because they were miserable in them. I asked them to take the time to deeply think what is it that they would like to do, something that will make them wake up each morning excited for the work they have to do. I suggested self-development courses and books for them to read. I was already doing that myself and had a good sense of how to guide them. It took Tarek three months to realize he had a passion for the furniture industry, which ironically is his father's business. Dena is an artist who paints beautifully. However, Dena lacked confidence in her skills. I kept encouraging her to build her confidence until she became the artist today that is admired by many people for her gifted talent, including her art teacher.

Nancy is a proud mom of two millennial girls. She told me that she had her first child when she was in her mid-thirties. She and her husband had great jobs and were paid generously. They started saving for their children's college before they were born. They were able to put them through college, which helped their children to be debt free when they started their careers. At the same time, because of their professional connections, they were able to get their children internships that led to great jobs. Her children are currently in their late twenties and still living at home because they love their parents. When I was talking with Nancy, one of her daughters was home, and she jumped in and responded to some of my questions supporting what her mother was saying. So, it could be that millennial parents are good parents, and their children like to stick around, not because they are a spoiled generation.

I asked Daniel if he liked his children to stay home or if he wanted them to move out. I was surprised when he said, *"I like them to stay home. One of my sons still lives with us, and he is thirty years old!"* His son has a good career and no student loans. But Daniel did say that rent in the Washington

D.C. area was so high that a big chunk of the millennials' salary goes to rent and bills. I asked Daniel if our parents were more excited for us to move out; he told me that he was excited to move out and couldn't wait.

As a single mother, I lived my life for my children until I realized that my responsibility ended once they entered the workforce. However, I still wanted to be that mother, and I enjoyed it to many degrees. Even when sometimes I got stressed about the endless role of being a mother, I couldn't turn my back and set them free from my mind and heart. It was my choice, and no one forced me to be that mother. Today, when I look at my children, I don't see them as spoiled at all. I built a generation of good children who serve their community with high ethics.

As I mentioned, I consider Bob Proctor to be my mentor and idol. The first seminar I took with Proctor in 2017 was titled "Paradigm Shift." I couldn't go in person to Los Angeles to attend the seminar, so I participated in the live streaming. The three days of the seminar shifted my mind and my thinking. I felt as if I had discovered something no one knew.

Proctor gave us access to the seminar for about three weeks, and I shared the link with my children hoping they would watch it. It took lots of effort on my end to get them interested, but once Tarek listened to the streaming, he became obsessed. From then on, he started reading many books that Proctor recommended during the seminar. After the seminar, I contacted Proctor and Gallagher Institute requesting to learn about more courses. I ended up enrolling in a thirteen-month coaching program, where I would study many books and topics, and I had access to unlimited audios that support the materials in the program.

My children started noticing the change in me, and they liked it. First, they noticed how calm I had become and how I spent so much time reading and listening to audios. Second, they saw a happy mother who is always in a good mood and inspiring when she talks. They started enjoying talking to me more and listening to the things I was learning. Eventually, my children began studying with me. They too started changing and setting goals for themselves. Since then, we have not stopped working on our self-development, and now we can find so much to talk about. They even started recommending books to me and sending me articles to read. I never had that type of relationship in my youth with my parents; I don't think we even talked about anything other than giving chores and orders. To see that this generation wants to learn and grow is fantastic.

Then I started sharing the information I am learning with other millennials I became friends with throughout my jobs. Sandy worked hard on her self-development until she figured out what her passion was. One day she came to visit, and she started telling me that she has a strong passion for health and fitness, and she wants to enroll in a course to become certified. She was concerned about the cost of the course and if she would be able to manage her time between studying, a full-time job, and a weekend job. We discussed her options and abilities for a few hours, and at the end, she said to me, "*you truly inspired me. I want to go home and sign up for the course. I believe I can do it.*" She sure did. Today, I can only say how proud I am of Sandy. She is doing what she loves, and so many other opportunities opened up for her that she told me, "*I feel as if I am dreaming.*"

My children love each other and support each other in dire situations. Natalie grew up without a father. Tarek is nine years older than she is, and he played the role of a father figure and older brother. Natalie looks up to Tarek as a role model, and he sure is a good child and a good example for a brother. If Natalie did not do well in one of her classes in school, she would be so concerned about what Tarek might say or if he would be disappointed in her. I don't think she gave a crap about what I might have thought as much as she did about Tarek. Instead of feeling jealous, I played along by using Tarek to get a point to Natalie that I failed to get through or I needed support to my argument. It worked perfectly. Even today, Natalie is 19 years old, and she still cares what he thinks of her.

One day, Natalie wanted to get a tattoo. I hate tattoos, and I am so against them since I don't like the idea of marking my body with a permanent mark. Neither one of my other children ever considered a tattoo, which made it hard for me to know what to do in Natalie's situation. She argued that she was nineteen and could make her own decision. I felt hurt to hear that a few months ago, when she was dependent, I needed to make all the decisions, but once she turned eighteen on paper, I was no longer in charge. I looked at Natalie sternly and said to her, "*If you can make your decisions because you are nineteen, then go make all your decisions on your own, and don't come to me about anything.*" I walked upstairs to my room feeling disappointed as if nothing I had done in my life mattered anymore once my children turned a certain age.

A couple of months went by, and Natalie opened the topic of a tattoo again but this time in a tricky way. We both were sitting at the ophthalmologist clinic waiting for my turn, when Natalie showed me on her phone a quote that says, "wherever there is love, there is peace." She knows I love those type of quotes because I am a big believer in peace, so I said to her, *"that is a beautiful quote."* Then she showed me on her phone the same quote but in the Arabic language. I am of Middle Eastern origin and read Arabic well. I read it and said to her, *"wow, the translation is so perfect that even in Arabic it sounds powerful."* She had a big grin on her face and said to me, *"that will be my tattoo."* Darn, I fell in the trap, and she made it sound as if I approved of the tattoo. I looked at her with a frown and said, *"Put the tattoo on your ass."*

Natalie called her brother a few days later and told him about the tattoo that she wanted to do in Arabic and that it meant a lot to her because Mommy loved the quote. Tarek was unhappy about the idea of her getting a tattoo and asked her to reconsider and not do it so she could be cool in front of her friends. They went back and forth with the discussion, and eventually, Natalie got frustrated and told me that her brother is old-fashioned. That night, Tarek and I were talking on the phone, and at the end of the call, he asked me if I was fine with Natalie getting a tattoo. I told him, *"no, I never told her that, but she is going to do it anyway, so I don't have much of a say."*

Natalie took a few days, pretending she thought the idea over based on Tarek's request. Then she texted him and said that she still wanted to go ahead with it, and she hoped he would support her. Of course, he gave in and told her that it was her decision at the end of the day. Natalie had the tattoo on her bone collar, and I tell you, it looked beautiful, but of course, I told her it looked ugly. I cannot deny that deep inside of me, I knew that she did everything possible to get our approval and cared about what we, as her family, thought.

Parents of millennials kept their children's lives busily structured with sports, music lessons, club meetings, youth group activities, and part-time jobs, according to research by Linda B. Nilsson. Nowadays, we can keep an eye on our children through social media. I know where Natalie is from her SnapChats. I never cared to use SnapChat, but she taught me to how to use it, and I ended up on it to see my children's photos and stories. Even through social media, I know who their friends are, and I can stalk her friends to know more about them. This is a luxury my parents did not have, and I bet if we ever sat in an honest session, they would be shocked as hell to learn of the things we used to do behind their backs. That being said, it does not mean today's parents know everything their children are doing, but it sure helps a lot.

Daniel told me that he didn't have serious issues with his children, but he was always concerned about them getting involved in drugs. He kept a close lookout and encouraged them to spend time playing sports to make sure they were doing something productive with their time.

John told me that he was involved in his children's activities but also monitored their social lives. He had lived in his house since his two boys were born, and they knew the neighbors well. His boys went to school with the neighbors' kids, who also were their friends. John did admit that he stalked his children on social media to make sure they were hanging around the right group and not getting in trouble.

One day I saw Natalie's SnapChat that showed one of her male friends driving my car. When she came home, I gave her one option only—if she ever volunteered my car for anyone to drive, from her friends to the neighbors to the extended family, she should prepare to start walking everywhere. It was then I realized that I should give her credit for being so open on social media knowing I am on it. She truly is a good kid and honest. She taught me that the iPhone allows us to share our locations and that way I would always know where she was. This gave me a sense of relief to know where she was, especially late at night or when the weather was bad. Transparency does lead to trust, and now I find myself hardly checking Natalie's location unless something worries me, or if I text her and she does not respond for a while.

During my era, many parents couldn't wait until their children turned eighteen, to leave the house and go their way. My generation, without today's technology, was able to make it on our own, even without parental support yet with a lot of struggle. We learned as we went in life with minimum support. The only communication we had was a landline or mail. How did we become such caring parents? Could it be because of the independent life we lived? Sarah Kendzior, the author of *The Art of Parenting*, described the concept of a "helicopter parent" as someone who "micromanages every aspect of his child's routine and behavior. From educational products for infants to concerned calls to professors in adulthood. Helicopter parents ensure their child is on a path to success by paving it for them."

A *Huff Post* article, by Haydn Shaw, shows how much helicopter parenting exceeded its limits. Shaw says, "*We have all seen those parents who constantly hover over their child and then jump to rescue them when a soccer coach doesn't play them enough or a teacher gives their report a C grade. We can tell which science fair projects the parents did for their kids.*" Shaw says that helicopter parents' role does not end when their children graduate from college; they can go as far as calling or writing the human resources department to argue that their child should have received the internship or promotion. He even said they play a similar role at work as they did when their children were in school by calling the boss and explaining why their child couldn't come into work.

I have not witnessed such situations at any of my jobs where parents interfere in their children's professional life. However, I went through a similar situation once with Tarek. My intention was not to baby my son, who was twenty-four at that time. One day, Tarek got sick with strep throat. He was working as a waiter in a restaurant, and he needed to be at work that morning. His condition was serious with a high fever, and he was hallucinating. He couldn't get up to go to work or even call in sick. He needed the job until he found a job in his degree field, but meanwhile, he was working long shifts as a waiter to earn some income. I was concerned about him losing his job if he didn't call in sick. Restaurants find it difficult when a waiter doesn't show up to do his shift, and they do not always have enough people on the floor to cover up in case someone did not show up. I thought of doing both my son and the restaurant a favor by calling in and giving his manager a heads up, hoping I gave her enough notice to find a backup for his shift.

When finally I was connected with the manager, whom I had never met, I introduced myself as Tarek's mother. As soon as I did that, I could sense that she had become cold on the other end of the line. At that moment, it hit me that I was treating my son as if he were a child in school and that I had made a mistake by calling his manager. I wanted to hang up quickly, but it was too late, so I said to her, "I wouldn't be the one calling you if Tarek was able to. He is so sick with a high fever, and he will not be able to come to work today." She responded in a bossy tone: "Ma'am, tell your son to call me himself, or he doesn't need to come back to work ever."

I was dumbfounded. I knew my son had lost his job, and not only was he going to be devastated by the loss of income, but he also was struggling to get a job after he graduated from college. By evening when he was able to get up for a bit, I told him what his manager said, and he said, *"fine, she did me a favor. I never liked working with her anyway."* I honestly did not blame him.

Tarek is a responsible man and has high work ethics. His previous manager liked him and knew during his shift that they could rely on him running the floor on his own. But to be so judgmental based on one incident, I felt was unfair. Tarek never went back to work after this incident, and he was able to find another job that turned out much better. After a few months, Tarek heard that the manager in his old job was laid off for various reasons, but I wanted to console myself by believing it was karma.

In a different situation, Tarek had to take me to the emergency room one night. I was scheduled for surgery in a few hours, and the first thing that I asked Tarek to do was to call my manager and tell her. My manager was very understanding and supportive. She stayed in touch with Tarek through the phone checking on me until she made sure I was doing well.

Ordinarily, I would never put my children in an embarrassing situation where I would call their boss to give her a piece of my mind about why she mistreated my child, although, in my head many times, I *wished* I could do it. I did, however, spend hours discussing with my children the situation he or she was facing at work, hoping I could be of help. This was something I missed in my young life, to have parents that I could go to for advice about life, about careers, and studies. So I wanted to do it for my children. I do not see an issue of being a mentor to one's children in their career life as long as the parent does not tell the adult child exactly what they should do and if they do not do it, the parent gets upset. I give my two cents and leave the action to them. If my children do not trust my judgment, they will not come to me. They will go to someone else whether it is a friend or another family member.

I feel sorry for children that have parents that embarrass them. Shaw says in his article that some parents request to go with their children to the job interview. He said that an international pharmaceutical company told him that young applicants asked to bring their parents to the interview often enough that they had to create a standardized company response. Parents, if you are one of them, please don't do this to your children. They are not in school anymore, and you not only embarrass them, but I doubt they would be considered for the position or any other job. Who the heck would want to hire a baby?

It varies from individual to another based on how their parents think. There are the type of parents that decide for their kids what they believe is right for them. There are parents that let their kids decide, but they give them advice and make sure their children are ready to make the right choice. Most common is that parents have expectations for their kids that can be unrealistic sometimes and drive millennials to be stressed about every step they make in life. Millennials tend to please their parents for reasons only they know of, but I can guess from a few discussions with millennials that they are worried about making their parents upset. Or they are concerned their parents will not take care of them financially if they do not do what is expected of them.

Tarek believes that his generation, in general, is not raised to make decisions. He said to me that parents of millennials seem to influence their children up to college, and once millennials reach adulthood, they find themselves lost and unequipped to make their own decisions. He said, "*We, as a generation, are not trained to think on our own, and when it is time to decide our future, such as selecting classes in college or applying for jobs, we don't know how to make the right decision.*"

Natalie said, "*When you are out of high school, you still feel like a baby under your parents' rule. We do go by what they want in the beginning, but once we start college, our parents see us like grownups, and we are on our own.*" She elaborated how millennials in college have to learn how to manage their schedule, pick up their classes, and decide what to eat and other daily matters. Millennials realize they have become adults, and their parents don't choose everything for them anymore. Sandy told me that her parents wanted to accomplish their dreams through her, which adds pressure on her, and she feels she should not disappoint them. She told me that she is always stressed out from the fear of letting her parents down. Her parents did not get the opportunity to go to college, so they wanted her to go to college and do her master's right after undergraduate school. Continuing her education was not her choice, but Sandy seemed to see the benefit of it after she graduated. She said, "*I'm glad they pushed me to pursue my higher education right after I graduated from undergrad, but sometimes I wonder if I had taken a few years off and gained experience, would I have made a better decision?*"

Many millennial parents tend to overprotect their children by hiding information from them thinking they do not need to know or stress about things. Parents could be unhappy in their marriage, and their children do not feel it until they are shocked by the news that their parents are getting separated or divorced. At home, parents may not discuss much in front of the children except what brings them to a bright future. Parents seem to forget that millennials understand what is going on around them and in the world through social media. Nothing is hidden from millennials nowadays, and neither should the parents be hiding things.

Communication was a useful tool I used with my children since they were very young. Teaching them right from wrong by engaging them in a discussion worked better than using punishment or getting upset by them. I do get upset by certain behaviors my children display especially when I know they know they could do better. But I do my best to explain to them why specific actions or behaviors are wrong from my point of view. I taught my children to be critical thinkers and see the big picture rather than limit their vision to a specific point. I also taught them to think of options as solutions and narrow down to the best option. I love having options. I see options as a backup plan, and it makes me comfortable knowing if this plan does not work out, I still have other options to try.

I also raised my children to think of solutions rather problems. Our innate reaction as humans to any problem is to get upset and nervous and stop reasoning. Once you put the problem aside and start thinking of solutions, you feel empowered instead of helpless. This is a skill our children will carry with them in life, and it will help them deal with different situations whether professional or personal. We prepare our children to be leaders in anything they do. They eventually, if they haven't already, want to have a family of their own. It is good to give them the skills to raise a good generation. There is no way on earth I want to be the grandmother who is still raising kids for my kids. I fell into that trap with their pets when they brought their dogs home and asked me to sit for a few hours, and the few hours turned into a full day and sometimes night. I told my kids, *"when you plan on having children, give me a heads up so I can move as far as possible from you."* This is when I did my best as a parent but then had to cut and run and let my adult kids deal with matters on their own. Why should we spend thirty years of our lives raising our children and then raise them and their children?

I think it is important to hear out millennials about how they see their relationships with their parents and vice versa. Millennials are confused about their relationships with their parents. In my interviews, I could sense their love for their parents and the desire to please them and not make them upset. At the same time, they are frustrated that their parents cannot let go of them and give them independence.

The millennials I spoke with feel torn between their parents and the reality of their era. Socially, the millennial generation is more open-minded than the previous generations. Many embrace the legalization of medical marijuana in a number of states and recreational marijuana in nine states and Washington D.C., and the legalization of same-sex marriage. History broke barriers that many baby boomers would not have seen as possible when they were growing up. So much is happening on the political, economic, and social levels that the parents need to meet their millennial children halfway.

Natalie gave an example of how her parents grew up during racism and segregation, and she grew up hearing that from them. Then she faced the real world of her generation where the President of the United States was a black man. "*No one is born racist. We love who we want,*" Natalie said. She looked me in the eye and said, "*do I follow my parents or what is common right now? Who is going to teach me?*" I thought she was asking me, but then she responded to her question "*I have to teach myself because my parents are unable to.*" I thought that was powerful to hear from a nineteen-year-old. She is voicing the notion that parents need to wake up to the reality of today and raise their kids with that understanding, especially of the fact that life is changing and progressing so rapidly.

In *Millionaire Success Habits*, by Dean Graziosi, he talks about how this generation gets nothing but negative news through media. He explained how in the 1950s, *Time Magazine* covered 90 percent positive news. Then they realized people were more attracted to reading negative news, and they started posting more negative articles and sold more copies. Today's news is all negative, and they fill people's mind with news about murder, wars, conspiracies, economic crisis and terrorist activities that make a person just want to stay home to feel safe. As parents, we freak out from such news over our children and wish they could stay under our control so we can protect them and keep them safe. I used to be addicted to news and would watch different news channels each day to learn what was happening around me and in the world. I did it because I did not want to be ignorant and miss breaking news. I was always feeling scared and overwhelmed about everything, and I would imagine the worst was going to happen. If I heard sirens outside, I would instantly start wondering if my kids were safe. I reached a point where I was becoming tense and would panic from any news I heard on TV.

Then one day I decided to quit watching any news channels. My time became more productive, and I started reading often, especially positive books. I became less stressed and concerned about the wellbeing of my children, and I started believing the world around me was safe. Even my children were influenced by news because when they walked into the house, they would find me mesmerized in front of the TV. Of course, I would share with them the bad things I just heard. Once I stopped listening to the news, so did my children, and we started spending more time talking as a family about interesting topics.

Millennials are more open-minded than their parents' generation because they were introduced to the world through the screen of their laptops and smartphones. The millennials I interviewed and spoke with all loved their parents but do not feel connected on life matters. The culture in this new era is different, and millennials do not know how to share it with their parents without being judgmental and being judged. Millennials become secretive with their parents and as Natalie put it: "*The secret life millennials live with their parents made them secretive in their life overall. Even among each other, millennials do not share much.*" She added, "*We do not talk about details with each other because we become isolated individuals.*" It seems that millennials see that their generation has become more open and their parents are becoming more conservative, which created a bad transition between the two generations. Natalie said, "*No matter how cool your parent is, you are still unsure of what you share with them because of the age difference.*"

In my generation, parents used to get married young. Then the generations after started getting married later, and the age gap between the child and the parents became bigger. On the other hand, in all of the past generations, the children had an issue communicating with their parents because of the generation gap. I believe parents nowadays are more modern thinking than they were during my parents' generation.

During my generation, homosexuals came out in the open and started being accepted way more than they were during my parents' generation. Although there is still racism in the U.S., it is better now than it was during my time. We had a black president for the first time in our history; we had women running for the presidency in the United States. Canada, Britain, and several other countries have had female prime ministers. Interracial marriages are considered normal now whereas twenty or more years ago, someone might stare at an interracial couple. Younger people are also cautious about their use of language whereas the boomers inadvertently used all kinds of politically incorrect, offensive phrases that millennials will not use now because of a greater awareness of what could potentially be hurtful to another person.

When I was chatting with Sher, a millennial of thirty years old, she told me that she could not communicate with her parents about serious issues. They would change the topic immediately as if denying it in the hope that it would go away. She said, *"we would be eating dinner and chatting and I would ask a question about a tragic incident that happened to me when I was a child, and my mom would say, 'Honey, can you please pass the potatoes?'"* That would be the end of discussion. Sher is saying that sometimes parents do not want to deal with problems, and by avoiding them, they believe they are doing the right thing. She said she grew up that way where serious personal topics were not discussed as a family. This leads to trust issues. If my parents do not trust me, then I am not going to trust them. Millennials feel there is a cut-off line of how much they can share with their parents, and they stop there.

The technological development that rose during the millennial generation also created a gap with their parents' generation especially because many of them could not catch up with the new technology. Today, one is considered illiterate based on his or her savviness or lack of it to technology. This gap makes many, but not all, millennials distant from their parents, and they may not communicate much. They might become more secretive from their parents and in turn, this affects millennials' relation with their peers where they become secretive with each other. They are scared to share things with their friends in case parents find out. This is why they say millennials are strange and they spend all their time on their phones because at home, they become very sheltered and hidden.

# CHAPTER 11

## Baby Boomers

## Who Are the Baby Boomers?

*I* can speak firsthand on this topic being a baby boomer myself. I lived and learned from many generations including my parents and my children. Previous to the baby boomer generation, the generations of our parents were similar in many ways. That doesn't mean we, as their children, did not feel the gap, but it was mostly about cultural things. Baby boomers were becoming more liberal-minded than their parents, and there was the struggle of becoming independent from our parents' mentality. However, the gap was not as big as the gap between baby boomers and millennials.

Millennials' time is moving so fast that it is hard for baby boomers to grasp the changes and accommodate quickly. So, we end up moving in slow motion, still struggling to let go of our old-minded ways, whereas millennials are a new lively generation that is continuously speeding to catch up with the changes in their time.

Education during my parents' era was not always a common thing, and usually only those who came from well-off families had the opportunity to finish high school or college. My father was one of the lucky ones of his generation who went to college and earned a master's degree in chemical engineering. My mother barely made it to high school, but she loved reading especially history and politics. I used to call her 'the encyclopedia' because she could talk about any historical subject and give accurate dates.

Yes, I used to listen to her a lot and would open the encyclopedia to check the dates she gave me and would find myself in awe at how accurate she was.

Baby boomers had better educational opportunities than previous generations. Colleges were much cheaper than today's tuition, and people did not rely on student loans. I'm not sure if baby boomers invested in their children's education because they were educated or because they also were exposed to technology at a later stage in life or both. But I believe baby boomers did their best to care for their children and ensure they have a secure future with opportunities.

Understanding how the baby boomers' time was all about typewriters is helpful for millennials to see the technological level of that time and how different it was. I remember when I was in school, typing classes on a manual typewriter were a requisite. We all had to learn how to type, and that is what made us qualified over each other. Female baby boomers invested in their typing skills because the jobs that were available for us were secretarial positions unless a person studied medicine, engineering, or law. There were few of these women in the '60s and '70s, and the majority of them were secretaries, nurses, or social workers if they had white-collar jobs. Otherwise, women were waitresses, factory workers, and house cleaners. The options for women today are innumerable in comparison.

I recall when I first saw the electric typewriter how fascinated I was with it. I struggled, in the beginning, to control the speed of the keyboard and found myself making more typing mistakes than when using the manual typewriter that was hard to push on the buttons. It is similar to driving a stick shift, and then sitting behind an automatic transmission. At first, one would struggle with his or her feet because she or he adapted for so many years using two feet to run a stick shift car.

The skills that baby boomer women were proud of were their typing skills. I used to spend much of my breaks in high school sitting in the typewriter room, and practicing speed with accuracy. Typing is a skill as much as it is to play the guitar or any other musical instrument. In addition to mastering the speed with accuracy, we had to master typing without looking at the typewriter. I remember how I used to imagine I was blind and needed to type my research for school. I would close my eyes and feel the keys of the typewriter until my hands were able to sit right and move musically on their own. When women would apply for a job in those days, the most important thing to highlight on a resume was the speed of typing per minute. Nowadays, this skill is not only irrelevant, but people look at me as if I am weird typing with both hands. Nowadays, it is cool to type with two fingers on a cell phone and as fast as sixty words per minute. That I find a challenge for me from placing two hands on a keyboard to using two fingers on the tiny phone screen.

We were the first generation that was introduced to a box called a computer. It was an advanced typewriter with a screen, and that's what we used until the '90s when the Internet was connected. Then we had a computer with not only word-processing abilities but also the ability to search online and do so much more. I testify that I learned technology way before my kids did. I knew how to use Microsoft Office when my children had no clue how to use it.

I saw a cute post that said, "Okay, so you are 10 years old, you have a laptop, iPad, Facebook an iPhone… Dude, when I was 10, I only had one thing to play with… It was called OUTSIDE." I loved it because it summarized the difference between millennials and generations before them. Even when my millennial children were born, technology was not that advanced. They did get the chance to play outside more than late millennials.

## Baby Boomers' Work Ethics

Today the baby boomers work with the same mentality they were raised. Work in a secure job from 9-5 to get benefits and save for retirement. Whereas, the millennials laugh at the benefits and say who cares? They won't consider working for a corporation that does not have a union because to them that sounds fishy. Why do they need to work forty to fifty years when they have so many more opportunities than the baby boomers had? Did we have online shopping? Could we pay our bills online? I remember having to drive to the telephone company to pay my bills or mail them the check.

Repeatedly I heard from baby boomers, at my different jobs, that the millennials do not know what they want. They work two years maximum, and they get bored and start looking for a new opportunity. That is true. In my generation, we grew up learning that we should stick to a job until we retired. If we changed jobs during my time, people would have thought something was wrong with us. We liked our comfort zone as baby boomers and convinced ourselves that constituted stability. We wanted to grow in the same job and accrue a good retirement plan. Now, let me tell you my thoughts: it is insane to work forty to fifty years so that I can retire in my sixties and enjoy my life. I worked as an advocate for elderly people in long-term facilities for two years. I kept telling myself each day, is this what I want to retire for? Work my butt off so I can have enough money to pay for care? Heck, no. I want to live my life now and enjoy it. I don't mind being thrown in a dumpster when I am too old to take care of myself as long as I go satisfied.

Many baby boomers today are working under much younger people than they are. Every year, the requirement of having a "fresh outlook" is driving more highly sophisticated and high baby boomer performers aside. When they see that a millennial is being prioritized over them, even though they are years ahead in experience and knowledge, they feel deprived. According to a ProPublica report that addressed a headline, which goes like "Cutting 'Old Heads' at IBM," IBM specifically targeted older employees to be laid off even though they were perfectly well suited and ideal for the job. This doesn't mean that baby boomers have a negative perception of how the millennials are getting "age" benefits when it comes to climbing up the corporate ladder or even landing jobs. Baby boomers, however, do feel that the millennials have the upper hand because of being accustomed to the technology and techniques that they are now struggling to learn. With technology being the only upper hand for millennials, baby boomers feel that they can still hang on longer if they become accustomed and adapted to it too.

Baby boomers want to be recognized and appreciated. They are great leaders, and they want to be given credit for that. They feel that the millennials lack that explicit knowledge that they have, and it is a little harder to teach this knowledge to a millennial when one knows that they are going to be hired for *cheap* to do their jobs. This creates a barrier in the communication and transfer of that valuable knowledge. In the past, when a young one needed to be taught a great skill, they would first be required to become an apprentice and learn alongside the old. This doesn't happen anymore and is creating a big gap between the two generations.

Millennials often find it hard working with an old-fashioned generation that does not get them or meet their professional standards. They respect authority and fear standing up to older people, which is why they choose to quit jobs rather than address the issues.

I recall in one of my jobs, our previous president was very old school. He never believed in teleworking and wanted the staff to be present in the office five days a week. Even on bad snow days, when media was alerting people to stay home, he would be in the office expecting staff to be there too. The young staff wanted flexibility in their schedules. Once a new president arrived with a more modern approach, and he encouraged teleworking, there was a marked change in culture in the office. Young staff became happier at work and turnover of staff decreased. Of course, this isn't the only reason for the decrease, but he also managed to make other changes that made the staff happier. The president was in his fifties, but he understood how to make the workplace better. He bridged the gap between the two generations by taking simple actions.

I believe baby boomers and Generation X need to open their minds and become more accepting of working with millennials side by side. Just as we are proud to see our children succeed in their careers, we should also be happy to see the young employees growing and developing. Our job is to lend them a hand by teaching them the skills they need to be the next generation in control. As managers, we should coach and mentor young employees to bring in assets, not only to the workplace but also to the country overall.

Millennials have an excellent opportunity to learn from the older generations. They are rich in knowledge, which provides millennials with a blessed opportunity to take from them as much knowledge as possible. They have been around much longer, and have a lot to share. Millennials need to be open-minded and learn from anyone who can take them to the next level. If both generations look at it as a hands-off experience, they will work great together. Companies spend billions of dollars in North America training their staff each year. I believe if managers are better equipped, they will save their companies lots of money by providing in-house training from their existing experienced staff.

Working as a team with the objective of getting our companies to grow and succeed is what we all aim for. We all, regardless of age, experience, or which generation we come from, have something to add. When companies integrate modern with old, a bridge of knowledge is built.

# CHAPTER 12

## *My Two Cents: Tips for Millennials*

*I* don't have a magic wand to make your life perfect. I will leave that up to you, the reader, to decide how you want to go about it. Change is personal, and only you can make the changes that you want. What I can help with here is throughout my fifty plus years on this planet, I accumulated enough mistakes to learn from and experience to share. I never was afraid of making mistakes, and I sure made plenty of them. Today, I look at my past life, and I realize this is what brought me here today to be able to mentor and coach my children and those that have an expanded mind and are ready for success.

Parents are a great source of knowledge, and it is worth listening to them. Our elderly have been around for a while, and you can benefit by what they went through and use it as a shortcut for yourself, if you are interested in learning. Then there is the other approach, which I also support, which is to learn as you go and build your own experience. As long as you are aware of your behavior and what results it is bringing to you, you can fix it along the way.

We gathered from the previous chapters and from the interviews that millennials give up fast and change jobs within an average of two years. I will not say you should stick to your job longer as the previous generations did because this might not apply to your generation or to the way you see things as they are right now. But I do believe, for your sake first, and for the sake of your coworkers, you would be well advised to try to understand the reasons why you want to change your job before you quit. Ask yourself, what did I do to work things out, and which of those things did not succeed? From what I have seen throughout my experience of working and mothering millennials, they tend to walk away from trouble instead of dealing with it. If you must quit your job, as a solution to your growth and unhappiness, take the time to understand what your ideal job is before you jump into another one.

In one of my previous jobs, there were many management and structural issues at the workplace, but not one millennial I've known tried to go to their manager, or higher up management, to address the issues. They either kept the frustration to themselves or gossiped about it with their other coworkers who shared the same issues. In the long run, this only led to more frustration and made choosing escape an easy way out. When I used to talk to those who were quitting, I would encourage them to take part in an exit interview to tell HR honestly why they were quitting so that they could help improve the conditions for those who were staying. However, most of them responded to me, "I don't care. I am leaving."

Remember that speaking up benefits the person who comes after you. Even if you hate conflict and you have trouble being assertive, summon the courage to speak your mind. You could help so many people and organizations, starting with managers, who may have no idea of the details of what is going on in his or her organization.

Master problem solving. Never run away from your problems. There are solutions to every cause. The more you invest in solutions, the more joyful your future will be. Life is a skill, and you will acquire that skill by mastering it. The more you face the obstacles along the way, the more skilled you will be.

This includes difficulties in the workplace, although I recognize that some jobs have hostile environments and are toxic, in which case, you want to leave. Other times, there is a solution to working out your problems on the job. You may just have to think out-of-the-box to find it.

I remember a discussion with one woman who was gossiping the most and spreading her negativity around. Even those who had not yet started seeing the issues were influenced by her attitude. I asked her to say everything she told me to HR. I even told her how she could turn her anger into constructive criticism by giving her examples. She never did. It took the organization many years to realize the issues they were having and to address them gradually. When I left that same job, I prepared for my exit interview so well that not only did I share what I went through, but I also discussed what others shared with me. I criticized things in an organized manner, point by point, and said at the end, "I am leaving and not holding a grudge. I love this organization and believe in its mission. I am sharing this with you because I care, or else I would leave like all those before me and not say a word." The HR person thanked me very much and told me she was surprised that others did not share that with her.

I highly recommend that once you quit a job for another job, take a break between both jobs for at least a week, and try to think of the lessons you learned from the previous one and how you can do better at the new one. I don't mean better at your work, as if you were not doing a good job before. I mean communicate better with your managers even if you have to manage up by going above and beyond the tasks assigned to you so that you can enhance your manager's work. Managers respect strong employees who show interest and passion in their work. Two millennials I worked with had the guts to sit with their manager and open up about what was making them unhappy. One got promoted eventually because her manager saw her passion and efforts. The other one communicated her frustration in anger and blame so that the manager did not get the message about what the actual issues bothering her were. Instead, her manager saw that she was not fit to invest in because she would be quitting her job soon.

Losing your temper makes you look bad and does not do anything to solve the problem. You want to be aware. Feeling angry or frustrated is fine, but don't act it out. Express it verbally. You could change an entire organization for the better by doing so.

I believe if you choose quitting as a way out in your professional career, you will also apply the "quitting" formula in your relationships with your family, your significant other, your friends and other personal matters in life. Once you learn how to stand up for your rights and state your opinion in a calm manner, you will be heard.

Also, you millennials should stop comparing yourselves to your peers. This will be the beginning of ending the drive to move too fast just because others are ahead of you. Have confidence in who you are as an individual. You were created in a special, unique way. You do not need to follow the crowd or your peers. Be yourself and follow your heart and mind. Social media opened your eyes to more things, so that can make life confusing.

But what you see on social media is not the facts; it's been "filtered." It is hard to tell what goes on behind closed doors. People don't want to share their dirty laundry on social media. They want to show you their best. Sometimes that is good for them to believe in a good life that they dream of having and convince themselves through postings that they are living the ideal life. However, what is essential for you is to understand that you should go after the things that you want and not because it was induced in you for all the wrong reasons.

Go after what makes you happy, and be original instead of copying others' lives or spending your time being miserable about why you do not have what they have. Once you are living that beautiful life, no one needs to know about it. It is yours to enjoy. Unless you want to share your success for the sake of inspiring others, then go for it.

Always have goals. Written goals are preferable to verbal because people who write their goals down are much more likely to achieve success. Update your goals every few months because after you achieve them, you want to move on to accomplishing something else. Don't let anything distract you from achieving your goals. I wish I had known that when I was younger and taken advantage of opportunities. Goals get you excited to get up each day and look forward to doing something for yourself and your growth. Once I learned that, I have been producing immensely in my life. I saw how it helped my children when they started writing down goals. They became achievers. Today, my children accomplish a goal and set the next goal immediately. Once you start achieving your goals, you cannot stop. This applies to your personal and professional life.

Always work on your self-development. Take advantage of technology. You will find immense courses—some are free, and some are pricey, but they are worth your investment. I can't tell you how much I spent on self-development courses, and I have no regrets. On the contrary, this is what I will keep doing to the last drop. I know many millennials who listen to positive and good audios on Podcast. Once you set your mind, you will find the resources.

Also, reading is something beautiful. So many amazing books are out there that once you start, you will not stop. I always tell my children, "Books are your wealth; don't be cheap about spending money on them. They will bring health and wealth into your life." If you don't like the thought of sitting down on the couch or in a chair or lying in bed reading a book in print, read on your Kindle or Nook. Subscribe to audible.com, or load your MP3 player or iPhone with audio books so that you can be "reading" when you are taking a walk, working out at the gym, having a lunch break, etc. Reading makes you a well-rounded, more interesting individual. It can also be very entertaining and provide a wonderful escape.

Travel the world. There are countries and cultures on this planet that are beautiful. Your mind expands with travel and exposure to different cultures. You will change as a person and start accepting and understanding the world in a better way. The media has scarred our minds with stereotypes. Once you become diverse in your thinking, you will realize that what is being communicated to us through media is an exaggeration. You will develop the ability to think on your own without being guided. Don't forget the different foods you can try when you travel. It is true, we are a diverse country in the U.S., and we have food from different countries, but when you eat the food from the source, you will notice a huge difference from what we eat in the U.S. It is more authentic.

Be adventuresome. Never fear anything except what will make your conscience ache. Your conscience will not warn you ahead of time; it will let you do it and then torture you. Always think before you act. Always give the best in you, and do not wait for a reward. You will be rewarded for all the good you put out.

You are young, and the future is ahead of you. Don't waste time because you won't be young for long. Use your time in every useful way for yourself and your community.

Whatever you do, do out of love and commitment. Enjoy what you are doing, and don't drag for long on what you don't like. The same thing holds true with people. Those who stress you out and you can't find grounds to deal with, get away from them before you become like them. There are many negative people who don't want you to succeed because it reminds them of their failure. Remember those who are successful and left footprints for you to follow? That is who you should look up to.

Never fear life's turmoil. Look at it as a phase that teaches you lessons, and know that good is waiting ahead. Always learn from experiences, and review where you go astray. Fix your faults, or else you will carry them with you like a debt.

You will be parents yourselves, if you are not already. If you do not address the issues inside you, you will raise your children with your weaknesses; then they will learn to give up on things quickly. I'm sure you want a better life for your children than the one you had, so work on changing and growing to be a role model for your kids and the next generation.

When you are a parent, your children will criticize you too. Always remember yourself when you were their age, and take it from there. Don't forget you were like them once, and do not start acting like your parents, whom you are complaining about. Do better.

I want to end with Ellen DeGeneres' words when she ends her show: "Be kind to one another."

# Resources

Global Co Lab Network: https://www.globalcolab.net/

Proctor Gallagher Institute: http://www.proctorgallagher.institute/

Peggy McColl: http://peggymccoll.com/

My Millennials: www.mymillennialsbook.com

Nisreen Khalaf Thinking Into Results:
www.nisreenkhalaf.thinkingintoresults.com

# References

"Census Bureau Releases Comprehensive Analysis of Fast-Growing 90-and-Older Population", United States Census Bureau, November 17, 2011, [https://www.census.gov/newsroom/releases/archives/aging_population/cb11-194.html]

"Centenarian", Wikipedia, accessed October 5, 2018, [https://en.wikipedia.org/wiki/Centenarian]

"Death by Text Message? Stats Show How Technology Is Killing Us", Division of Motor Vehicle website, author Bridget Clerkin, published April 28, 2017, [https://www.dmv.org/articles/death-by-text-message-stats-show-how-technology-is-killing-us/]

"5 Ways Millennials View Healthcare Differently", UIC, accessed October 8, 2018, [https://healthinformatics.uic.edu/resources/articles/5-ways-millennials-view-healthcare-differently/]

"Generational Breakdown: Info about all of the Generations," The Center for Generational Kinetics, accessed September 27, 2018, [http://genhq.com/faq-info-about-generations/]

"Generation X—Not Millennials—Is Changing the Nature of Work", CNBC MAKEIT, published April 11, 2018, [https://www.cnbc.com/2018/04/11/generation-x--not-millennials--is-changing-the-nature-of-work.html]

"Just How Many Baby Boomers Are There?", Population Reference Bureau, accessed October 11, 2018, [https://www.prb.org/justhowmanybabyboomersarethere/]

"Led by Baby Boomers, Divorce Rates Climb for America's 50+ Population", Pew Research Center, article by Renee Stepler, March 9, 2017. [http://www.pewresearch.org/fact-tank/2017/03/09/led-by-baby-boomers-divorce-rates-climb-for-americas-50-population/]

"Millennials in the Workplace Training Video", YouTube, published by Official Comedy June 15, 2013, [https://www.youtube.com/watch?v=Sz0o9clVQu8]

"Millennials Outnumber Baby Boomers and Are Far More Diverse," United States Census Bureau, accessed October 9, 2018, [https://www.census.gov/newsroom/press-releases/2015/cb15-113.html]

"The Evolving Definition of Work-Life Balance", Forbes magazine website, contributor Alan Kohll, published March 27, 2018, [https://www.forbes.com/sites/alankohll/2018/03/27/the-evolving-definition-of-work-life-balance/#53faaefe9ed3]

"The Greatest Generation", Investopedia, accessed September 21, 2018, [https://www.investopedia.com/terms/t/the_greatest_generation.asp]

"The Millennial Generation Research Review", US Chamber of Commerce Foundation, November 12, 2012, [https://www.uschamberfoundation.org/reports/millennial-generation-research-review]

"The Six Living Generations in America," LinkedIn, published February 16, 2017, [https://www.linkedin.com/pulse/six-living-generations-america-vera-k-fischer]

"The Six Living Generations in America", Marketing Teacher, author Dr. Jill Novak, accessed October 11, 2018, [http://www.marketingteacher.com/the-six-living-generations-in-america/]

"The Work Habits of Millennials", Market Inspector, last updated August 3, 2018, [https://www.market-inspector.co.uk/blog/2017/03/the-work-habits-of-millennials]

"2016 Millennials Survey Highlights", Transamerica Center for Health Studies, accessed October 12, 2018, [https://www.transamericacenterforhealthstudies.org/health-care-research/2016-millennials-survey-highlights]

"Video Game Addiction No Fun," Web MD, accessed October 30, 2018, [https://www.webmd.com/mental-health/addiction/features/video-game-addiction-no-fun#1]

"Video Game Addiction Symptoms, Causes and Effects, PsychGuides.com, accessed October 31, 2018, [https://www.psychguides.com/guides/video-game-addiction-symptoms-causes-and-effects/]

"What Is a Millennial?", Metro News, published September 20, 2017, [https://metro.co.uk/2017/09/20/what-is-a-millennial-6942535/]

"Which Generation Is More Rebellious—Generation Y or the Baby Boomer Generation?", Quora, contributor James Wolfensberger, contributed February 9, 2014, [https://www.quora.com/Which-generation-is-more-rebellious-Generation-Y-or-the-Baby-Boomer-generation]

"Why Are So Many Baby Boomers Divorced?", CBS Evening News with Jeff Glor, article by Richard Schlesinger, December 14, 2010, [https://www.cbsnews.com/news/why-are-so-many-baby-boomers-divorced]

"Why Playing Video Games Can Actually Be Good for Your Health," Time, author Tessa Berenson, September 26, 2015, [http://time.com/4051113/why-playing-video-games-can-actually-be-good-for-your-health/]

"Why Video Games Can Be Good for You," Game Designing, accessed October 31, 2018, [https://www.gamedesigning.org/why-video-games-are-good/]

# About the Author

Nisreen Khalaf is a mother to three millennials, whom she has raised to challenge the status quo and go after what they want in life, believing that they each have too much potential to settle for an "average" job and lifestyle.

Nisreen has worked in nonprofit organizations for over 20 years in development and humanitarian aid. Her passion for people and desire to see a world full of hope and love compel her to focus on her career working for refugees. Currently, Nisreen works for an American organization as the Director of Humanitarian Aid and In-Kind providing various health, education, economic development and emergency responses to refugees in the Middle East region.

Nisreen is a Thinking Into Results facilitator and coach, who guides her client to achieve the success they so crave and to fulfill their dreams. Nisreen, who is intensely growth- and goal-oriented, helps individuals, groups, and companies discover their deepest goals and desires, reach their potential, and achieve their personal and professional goals.

She is particularly interested in working with millennials and has many years' experience coaching them to be their best selves.

Be sure to follow Nisreen on **www.mymillennialsbook.com** and at **www.nisreenkhalaf.thinkingintoresults.com**

# Connect with Nisreen Khalaf

**www.mymillennialsbook.com**

| | |
|---|---|
| Consultancy: | www.nisreenkhalaf.thinkingintoresults.com |
| Facebook: | https://www.facebook.com/mymillennials.book.7 |
| Instagram: | @mymillennialsbook |
| Pinterest: | https://www.pinterest.com/mymillennialsbook/ |
| Twitter: | @mymillennialsb1 |
| Email: | consultant@nisreenkhalaf.com |

# HEARTS to be HEARD

## Giving a Voice to Creativity!

Wouldn't you love to help the physically, spiritually,
and mentally challenged?

Would you like to make a difference
in a child's life?

Imagine giving them:
confidence; self-esteem; pride; and self-respect.
Perhaps a legacy that lives on.

You see, that's what we do.
We give a voice to the creativity in their hearts,
for those who would otherwise not be heard.

*Join us by going to*

## HeartstobeHeard.com

Help us, help others.

www.ingramcontent.com/pod-product-compliance
Lightning Source LLC
LaVergne TN
LVHW051240080426
835513LV00016B/1691